Rowing with my Wife

Rowing with my Wife

The Adventures of a Gig Rower

Dan Williams

SPORTS
BOOKS

Published by SportsBooks Ltd

Copyright: Dan Williams ©
April 2006

SportsBooks Limited
PO Box 422
Cheltenham
GL50 2YN
United Kingdom
Tel: 01242 256755
Fax: 01242 254694
e-mail   randall@sportsbooks.ltd.uk
Website www.sportsbooks.ltd.uk

Cover art by Martin Ursell

Typeset in Palatino LT Std

A CIP catalogue record for this book is available from the
British Library.

ISBN 1899807 36 5

Printed by Creative Print and Design, Wales

Dedication

For Anne, Genevieve and Claire

The members of Devoran Pilot Gig Club and the wider gig rowing community in general. With sincere thanks for letting me share with you in the exhilaration, pain and celebrations of gig rowing, the best sport in the world.

Contents

Acknowledgments

Firstly, to those sensible folk among you who asked, "haven't you got anything more useful to do?" The final answer is self evidently "No" and yes, I have kept the day job.

However, without the help and encouragement of a second group of misguided people this manuscript would never have reached fruition.

Next, a special acknowledgement is due to Claire White of Falmouth Gig Club for her invaluable help in the organisation and preparation of this manuscript. It was generous of you to give so freely of your time and knowledge.

My thanks are also due to Anne Tippett, for typing the early chapters, deciphering handwriting, described as "worse than a doctor's prescription notes", and to my mother for early proof reading; to my colleague Sue Leathley and her friend Bob Shelley for their encouragement and feedback, and to Cath Harvey, ever helpful if I needed a typist, a good cuppa, or a gee up to get on with it.

I would also like to record my appreciation for the help of several long-suffering members of Devoran Pilot Gig Club, especially Jezza, Nigel, Terry and Nikki, who were handed pages of manuscript at inopportune moments and then expected to provide POSITIVE feedback.

Finally, a huge thank you is due to my family, to Anne, Genevieve and Claire for typing duties and false smiles under pressure when Dad pointed to "a particularly amusing paragraph".

To my publisher. In retrospect, I really feel you should have gone with that story line I first proposed about that secret Catholic sect...

Disclaimer:

I have every confidence that all my dear colleagues and fellow club members will take my whimsical account of their exploits in good heart. However, just in case any of you fall on particularly hard times and do consider suing then the reference you will refer to is obviously fictional and anyway all the names have been changed!

(And my mate Colin is a solicitor, so there!)

Introduction

Approximately a decade ago I started to become aware that every New Year I was getting 'phone calls from old friends gently, but rather intrusively, enquiring into, "How I was". This was then followed by an enquiry as to Anne's state of mind and our ongoing marital relationship. Now, I have always presumed and expected a certain loyalty, consistency even, from my old chums and I couldn't understand this negative line of questioning. So, a few years ago I finally flipped and put Graham and Kate, my old university mates, on the spot.

"Look, what is it with this line of enquiry? Do you know something about Anne that I don't? Why does everyone seem so concerned about our relationship?"

Kate replied that I should hardly be surprised. In fact, I had even invited such concern by the type of personal comments I kept making in my Christmas cards. I thought for a moment, but nothing came to mind.

"So what is wrong with happy, bloody Christmas, then? Has it suddenly taken on a sinister meaning in this miserable secular world?"

A pause, before Kate replied, not I thought without a note of irritation; "Don't you remember Dan? A few years ago you wrote at the bottom of our card, 'Anne and I have started rowing.' The next year you followed this with 'Anne and I are rowing more regularly together, and Genevieve is getting involved'. And last year the alarming message was, 'Anne and I have just had a long weekend rowing on the Isles of Scilly.

11

We both came home completely exhausted and in need of rest and recuperation'.

"Now I don't know about you, but I am pretty sure that Graham and I wouldn't go on arguing like that year after year, without something having to give. To be honest Dan, it sounds like a nightmare. And what with Gen being dragged into it. Have you ever thought of Relate counselling? Some friends of ours in Oxford tried it and honestly it better than trying to… "

"Kate, Kate". I was aware that my voice was raised, "Oh, my God, I just never thought, I mean how could I have anticipated that you would read it like that? It's not like it seems, Kate … look, what else does R O W spell?"

So what to do this Christmas? Explain to all those other friends? Or see the funny side of it and milk it for all it's worth? Perhaps if I write that we regularly row with four other people, and that we are all members of a successful rowing club then the penny will drop. Or will a rowing club be interpreted by some city friends as a sort of book club for very cross and argumentative people? I look forward to more January 'phone calls!

While on the subject, I'd like to thank Anne and the institution of marriage for helping to provide the impetus for the completion of this manuscript. If I'd been unattached, I would have carried on a sports-loving, socialising, bachelor lifestyle without being driven to spend hours and days in a darkened room putting pen to paper. But when one has wider responsibilities and is confronted with the "things have to be done, unless we want the house to fall down around us" scenario, then a serious get out clause has to come into play. To me, the creative instinct is there to be respected, even

12

prioritised and I could always feel a chapter coming on when I heard the tiles falling off the roof or when the lawnmower was being dragged out of the shed. I'm pen in hand by the time Anne comes in from work. Her enquiry as to "how near is supper to being ready?" has to be met with a "sshh, I really must get this paragraph finished. Maybe then I will get the tin opener out and knock something up".

But remember Anne, I'm sure it will be worth it as I did promise you that flat in Greece with the royalties. But before you ask... I would like to lay the patio next weekend but I have just started a book on village cricket.

As my IT skills are somewhat on a par with Fred Flinstone's, Anne has been the subject of regular harassment as I attempt to cajole her into typing my handwritten notes. Not easy, as my chaotic scribbling has a spider-with-dysentery look about it. Imagine hundreds of your GP's prescription notes all running in to one another, and you are getting close. Having spent hours going through the "Dan is that a word or an involuntary hand movement?" exchanges, a creative solution was required. It arrived one Saturday morning in a big red box. Problem solved... divorce on hold... a voice-activated dictation system. Attach a few wires, load a disc, stick some headphones on and away you go. Fantastic. A novel a day and still time for last orders in the local.

Well, so much for the theory. Believe me, this software has a mind of its own. In fact, in many instances its output has been much funnier and more inventive than my input. For example, I dictated an innocent line about pulling the boat up the bank and it typed back something about 'Bank managers mating'. A few lines later it printed the word 'urinal' when I had clearly said the 'final'. It then came up with the word 'buffoon' of its own accord. Now I am really getting paranoid. It's getting personal!

Having a deep distrust of technology, I have a theory that there is now a higher being on the other side of the screen pursuing another agenda that is at total variance to my own. Perhaps, given a free rein, a surreal book about mating bank managers will emerge or a new series of Goon scripts.

So, it could well be that if you do find funny passages in the following two hundred or so pages they have been written randomly by my PC.

Bless you Anne, I haven't laughed so much for years.

I did read somewhere that you become somewhat of a hostage to fortune when you describe a book as 'humorous'. What's funny to one reader…

I have one friend, Sally, who never smiles at anything. A pessimist by nature, the sort of girl who if she smelled flowers would look around for the hearse. Now if I give her some of my stuff to read, I watch her face with interest (the way miners kept an eye on their canaries). If her face muscles move at all, then six marks out of ten for that passage. If her mouth twitches and cheek bones rise… I've done it… It must be bloody funny and as the saying goes, would "bring down the Palladium". Sally did actually laugh once, but that was during a passage about the monkey and the bank managers so I can't take the credit for that.

Still, at least with a directive adjective like 'humorous' you create a shared expectation. A friend and work colleague, Dr Denis Lawrence, recently published an academic text on dyslexia. This sold increasingly well in the UK and was subsequently translated into several other languages, including Korean. Denis happened to have Korean neighbours, and so lent the translation to them to gauge their response. A few weeks later, Mrs Choi called round and handed Denis back his book.

The verdict? "Oh Doctor Denis... very good... very, funny book. Thank you so much... we laugh so well". Denis did not know what to say as he couldn't think of a single passage that could possibly have ignited even a flicker of humour. So, what did they put in the translation?

So, maybe if I get this book translated into another language it will be interpreted as a sober, academic tome on the science of rowing. That way I'll have two bites at the cherry!

Finally, there is a saying that deep down within every one of us there is one great book waiting to get out. Judging by recent 'guttural' problems I believe mine remains lodged in my bowel area. In the meantime I can only offer you this superficial tour into the underbelly of a gig rower's world.

Pen Portraits

You will find many of the same characters appearing in the pages of this book. Below are some of the more prominent stalwarts of Devoran Pilot Gig Club.

Terry – barrel-chested, teak-hard, ex-miner. Body shaped similar to a firkin of Doombar bitter and rumoured to contain a similar amount of the amber-nectar. Bald of pate, generous nature with a smile the width of the Carrick Roads. On and off the water, a fighting spirit allied to steely determination. Dominates company with infectious laugh and back-slapping physicality. Up for anything and expects the same of others! Long-time captain and boatmaster. The spirit and soul of the club.

Anne – one of the more experienced, 'senior' female rowers; strong and committed competitor. Renowned for loud outlet of breath on 'in stroke' resulting in exhalation of spittle over coxswain (rabies discounted). Forceful coxswain and hay-tossing champion. Not to be trifled with... Rumoured to be kind to animals (still my wife at the time of writing).

Jezza/Jerry – think March Hare on speed. Hair style to match. Size of personality in inverse proportion to height, makes use of megaphone redundant; optimum listening distance 150 to 200 yards. Energetic, charismatic and generous to a fault. Seemingly known to everyone from Lands End to Bude (only tourists fail to give greeting).

Nigel P – tall, lean, experienced. Appearance, think

extra in Spaghetti Western. Alcohol intake indicated by width of smile and number of exposed teeth. An engineer by trade. Efficient and practical, the man to have on hand when the wheels come off the trailer. Never fails to check my ropy typing, so shrewd with a sense of self-preservation.

Nikki – Terry's wife. Long-time women's captain, now chairman. Coxswain respected and feared in equal measure. Has fought heroic but ultimately losing battle with club drinking culture. Now paid-up member of King Canute Society. Energetic table dancer (see Weymouth), famous for concluding evening of pole dancing by removal on stretcher.

Dr John – Well built, height restricted to medium through hair deficiency (think Marj Simpson for opposite effect). Since discovering that the body can survive life outside the 'comfort zone' has developed into a valued A crew rower. Self belief key to improved performance. Needs nurturing. Valued for good listening skills and sage advice. A party animal and impressive performer at the bar (but which medics aren't?). Needs to be loved. We love you John!

Brian – Impressive rowing physique, 8ft 10ins with shoulders to match. Huge potential, largely untapped. Intelligent, sociable and opinionated. Holds strident views on every subject from rowing technique to climate change. Invaluable choir master with resonant voice and total recall of every song ever written. Legendary drinker, who regularly hits double figures at the bar. Maintains health by, "not drinking at home". (But how can you be in two places at once Brian?). Intrigues club members with clandestine life-style. Could work for

MI5? Rowing commitments subject to distraction by exotic women. Needs to sort priorities and resume full-time training and socialising with his old mates.

Colin – subject of a chapter all of his own, see page 125.

Doombar bitter – Robust and full-bodied. Ideal companion after exertions on the water. Effect on rowers to promote conviviality, remove inhibitions (for those that had any) and encourage outbreaks of raucous singing. But beware, relationship prone to becoming obsessional and over familiarity can lead to impairment of senses and increasing instability. Essential component of Devoran PGC's training schedule and social bonding programme.

Chapter 1
Stroke What?

If 'no pain, no gain' is a realistic maxim then gig rowing is the perfect sport. Six bodies with 12 to 14 foot lengths of wood propel a 32-foot wooden boat through the water in whatever conditions nature can create as they are subjected to the verbal lashings of their cox. No fancy sliding seats, just benches and wooden rowlocks, known to gig rowers as thole pins (and occasionally called 'rollocks' for reasons that will become obvious later).

Definitely no stripy jackets or strawberries. In short, a man's game, most successfully in my observation survived by tough women with far more stamina than some of their more sedentary male counterparts.

So, how did a city boy, a landlocked cricketer, who was once sick on a ferry to the Isle of Wight, come to be grunting about through choppy seas off the Isles of Scilly competing in the grandly appointed, World Championship of Gig Rowing (1995)?

The beginning of the story started soon after Anne and I moved to Cornwall. One Sunday afternoon we were taking our regular Sunday stroll in Boscawen Park in Truro with our Dachshund, Fern. This led to a chance encounter with the closing stages of the Truro River Race.

Points of Interest
Truro River Race

Started by Truro River Rowing Club in the 1980s. In recent years the course has been lengthened, the start-line having been changed from Loe Beach to a point off Mylor harbour in the Carrick Roads, a mile or so east of Falmouth. This seven mile race is open to all forms of rowing craft and canoes, the start being staggered allowing the slowest boats to set off first. There are prizes for winners in each specific category. For pilot gigs the duration of the course is approximately an hour but this is very much dependent on the variations of the weather conditions. The finishing point remains just short of Tesco on the Truro city side of the Truro River. The boats then congregate and are pulled off the slipway at Boscawen Park.

As Anne and I were to come to appreciate, when the wind is against you this early season marathon can be a very challenging slog for the semi-fit.

It was a wild and windy day and as we crossed the park and approached the river bank section of the footpath I saw Fern nuzzling around a number of dark shadows that from a distance I mistook for fallen branches.

On closer inspection they turned out to be the retching bodies of the participants in the aftermath of this great rowing race. I remarked to one of the few vertical male crew on what a dreadful state many of his fellow rowers seemed to be in. He responded by merely pushing one of the girls off the path with his foot before expressing his empathy for their suffering.

"Well that's gig rowing for you. The wind was

against them and they obviously hadn't trained hard enough. They'll have to recover soon enough because the boats need loading up on the trailer".

Anne watched and listened attentively as Fern finished vigorously licking up the fluids that had been yakked up across the grass. Anne is a strange girl with a warped Protestant work ethic and an almost zealous and religiously penitent desire to suffer pain (perhaps marriage to me was the first step).

In short, a perfect match accrued. Anne took herself off to Truro Rowing Club's next training session and was soon a competitor in her own right, blistering her hands and rubbing her bottom away with the best of them.

Well good luck to her, each to their own... but I was a cricketer and definitely had better things to do on two evenings a week and on Saturdays than thrashing around in a wooden boat getting cold, wet and totally knackered. What could be the pleasure in that? While it is true that on a few occasions after accompanying Anne to the beach I was offered "a trial", I took a nano-second to decline.

As the end of March 1995 approached, Anne, excited about the prospect of rowing in her second World Championships in early May, confirmed that she had booked a week on the Isles of Scilly to accommodate the whole family. I looked forward to strolling between cafes and generally slobbing around on the beaches with the kids.

Then the 'phone call came... the captain of Truro Rowing Club. He outlined the situation. They had a problem, a B crew member had dropped out. No other rowers were available to go to the Scillies and the Championships were only six weeks away. They knew I was going; I had two arms and two legs, and well basically I had nine training sessions or less to learn to row!

After a long silence, I replied along the lines of: "Now, wait a minute. It's nice of you to ask but I really don't think I can help".

That was exactly 35 days before I rowed the first of ten World Championships!

It was to be a steep learning curve. On my first sortie I was directed to the front of the boat by an awesome female specimen in shiny Lycra. She sat in front of me, holding the rudder ropes and directed my legs between hers. The language of gig rowing is immediately rich with innuendo. "Do you want to stroke?" "Stroke what?" I naively enquired, wriggling my legs nearer to hers only to receive a withering stare.

The next instruction involved 'getting it in quickly', 'keeping it smooth' and 'pushing the last six inches'. I admit it took time to adjust my mental age beyond my shoe size as I concentrated with the others on pulling the oar out as long as I could.

Rowing your first race they say is what it's all about. As I was to find out, the contrast between paddling around the estuary as a 'novice' and racing three to four miles against hardened rival crews is about as great as entering a 13 month old toddler for a triathlon a few days after they have staggered their first steps. The early training is a cruel joke as 'racing' preparation but perhaps in retrospect the only way of encouraging normal human beings (exclude types like Anne) to keep returning.

To try and describe the physical sensation of gig

racing: imagine a ton of bricks on your chest, compressing and constricting your breathing; your leg muscles screaming under an effort similar to jacking up a small car and your arms and wrists being pulled out of their sockets by a force analogous to competing against the All Blacks tug-of-war team. This comes close.

It just reaches a point where you know you can't do it any longer and then the cox shouts one hundred yards to the first buoy (one third of the way around). At this point you can only pray for the intervention of an act of God or a freak of nature (a merciful tidal wave?). Throughout the race you are semi-conscious of a tirade of directions.

Why does the cox seems to be constantly shouting your name? "Come on Dan, more effort; rip it back, lay on it; come on more weight; give it everything".

You just think that there is nothing left to give when the cry goes up, "Right up for a big ten; after two; come on Dan, pull it to me, harder, more effort; give it to me".

At this point, I think I usually lose touch with reality in much the same way as I've read torture victims do. The body and the mind become disassociated.

And then I come round, lying face down on the beach, hyperventilating into slimy seaweed, gradually aware of the pins and needles shooting down my arms and legs, inclined to retch but lacking the energy.

The compensation you get?
- To enjoy a heightened appreciation of the time you aren't doing it. The banging-your-head-on-the-wall syndrome.
- The feeling that you've earned the beer you are about to drink in large quantities.
- To feel empathy with fellow sufferers – although I've

noticed that rowers in clubs that train properly skip out of the boat with oars aloft and walk up the beach in animated discussion – outrageous! It's supposed to be an amateur sport!

Points of Interest
Gig Specifications

Pilot gigs are 32 feet long rowing boats made to accommodate seven crew members; six rowers and a coxswain.

Second generation pilot gigs are all built to the same specifications, the template being the Treffry, a gig built by the Peters family for the Newquay club in the 1800s and considered the best of her time. A boat builder wishing to construct a new gig would now have to apply to the regulatory body, the Cornish Pilot Gig Association (CPGA), for a set of moulds. The traditional format would then have to be followed, inclusive of the use of elm planking, oak ribs and no laminations. The planking is overlapping, an example of clinker construction. During the building process the authenticity of the construction requires inspection by a representative of the CPGA.

Chapter 2
Ralph Bird

Former energetic rower, master boatbuilder, gig historian and author, Ralph Bird is a legend in the gig rowing community and in hot demand for his talks on *The History of Gig Rowing*. Ralph's slides have illuminated the paint-flaked walls of village halls from Sennen to Bude. History is brought to life as Ralph recounts discussions with gnarled old men who in their youth rowed to the aid of ship wrecks; fleshes out the story of the Saltash legend, Ann Glanville; brings to life the characters who reintroduced the sport of gig rowing and introduces champions from another age.

Ralph has met them or been witness to their stories through their relatives and his talks present a fascinating mix of factual and personal information. For example, at one point in his lecture Ralph informs us that one of the great boatbuilding family, the Peters from St Mawes, was called 'Tut Tut' Peters by locals due to his habit of shaking his head in disappointment and tutting if he smelt drink on the breath of colleagues. Like many Cornishmen of his time he was a devout Methodist.

Ralph's knowledge on the changing facets of gig construction is second to none. We learn that the beam width has varied by over a foot and the number of rowing positions could be anything from four to seven. Although now, under the present CPGA rules, exact conformity to the dimensions of the Treffry is enforced, Ralph explained that each boat still had their own characteristics in the water due to tiny variations and margins of error in construction.

Ralph has his own laconic style, announcing at the start of his talk, "Now this could take about two hours, so I am happy for you to go to sleep, plenty do. But could the loud snorers move towards the side of the hall, as one or two people may still be trying to listen".

I am in danger of becoming a Ralph Bird groupie, attending all the gigs; filtering the girls, rolling the spliffs, that sort of thing. But in RB's case it would be to carry the slide box and make sure a pint was always on hand to lubricate the larynx. I was very impressed with Ralph not needing notes even though he confirmed that in fact this was his 87th talk. Another thing in Ralph's favour is his pre-eminent knowledge level. If Ralph says that a hazy sepia picture is of the 18th century gig Tre-house that went aground off the Manicles while transporting a boat full of Tresco transvestites to a barn dance on Bryher then who are we to argue?

As I write, Ralph is preparing his 88th talk, but book early or you will be standing at the back as many of the audience return year after year, Bird enthusiasts who know a genuine rarity when they see one.

In 1981 Ralph organised the first contemporary gig races outside of the Newquay club. These were suitably called the Ralph Bird races. Saturday was a triangular course set off by Loe Beach in the Carrick Roads. The Sunday course was in the more sheltered waters of the Carrick Roads, from Turnahare Bar to the Pandora Inn. In 1984, Ralph founded Truro River Rowing Club who initially borrowed his gig, Energy. A few years later Ralph built their first gig, the Royal. The Royal and its crew was soon at the forefront of every race and remained a dominant force throughout the 1980s and 1990s.

Ralph was also a founding member of the Cornish Pilot Gig Association and a hugely influential and respected voice within it. But to the majority of gig rowers his legacy to the sport will always be the beautiful craft he has built and continues to build in his purpose-built shed in Devoran. Twenty-six gigs to date! A distinctive noise emenates from the shed, the noise of the planing and hammering being drowned by the sound of classical opera! (I know, Ralph, because I walk past so often).

Chapter 3
Call me Diego...

Following four years of rowing for Truro River Rowing Club, a long established, very successful and focused organisation, I switched my allegiance to Devoran Pilot Gig Club. Contrary to rumour, huge transfer incentives were not involved and Truro did not sign a five-page petition to try and stop me. Anne and I moved house from Truro, Cornwall's capital city, to the small village of Devoran. This is a community of a few hundred people situated equidistant between Truro and Falmouth on a tributary of the Fal Estuary. It now seemed sensible to carry on our sport within our new local community. For one thing this would fast track our acceptance as locals at the Old Quay Inn!

I suppose at this time in football terms this would have been analogous to moving from Manchester United to Plymouth Argyle. (Although admittedly with regard to the former I was only in the reserve team. More Diego Forlan than Ryan Giggs).

The year before Anne and I joined Devoran PGC they had made something of a name for themselves by crashing Helford's boat into the harbour wall at Newquay. To explain the context; it was on the first morning of the County Championships and a sharp north easterly was generating a big swell. Devoran, having been allocated Helford's gig from the pool of loaned boats, had just finished their race and were fighting their way back towards the shelter of the harbour. Just twenty yards or so from the entrance, a big wave picked up their stern, turned the boat sideways and drove her towards the granite wall. To the spectators' horror, a full-on collision ensued. Amid the sound of splintering wood, bodies were thrown into the swell.

The bow rower had been the first to encounter the unforgiving granite and some minutes later he was washed up onto the beach. He arrived semi-conscious and in a pool of blood. Colleagues and medics alike rushed to the scene, fearing for his life. Over the next few minutes, water was manually pumped from spongy lungs and stitches were inserted into a long, deep head wound. An immediate hospital visit was advocated followed by a prolonged period of rest and recuperation.

All sound advice and by anybody else it would have been dutifully (and very sensibly) followed. But the rower concerned was Terry Teague. No one who knows Terry, or Stan as he is also known, will be surprised by the outcome. Terry swore a few times, shook his head, got to his feet and headed back towards the harbour to gather up his crew and to prepare to row the next race.

The protest of doctors, organisers and loved ones were in vain. While he was still conscious and still capable of holding an oar, this ex-miner was not about to quit mid-championship and leave his team-mates short. All talk of imminent brain haemorrhaging was dismissed with a wave of the hand. To paraphrase Terry's logic, "look I'm getting in the boat. If it kills me, it kills me, but I'm responsible, and that's my choice".

Fortunately, Terry survived or, other considerations aside, the character and content of this book would be seriously diminished!

Two years later, Terry was rowing the same championship strapped up with broken ribs. But that is another story... one of many that inevitably seem to centre around the indestructible Devoran man.

Established by villagers in 1991, Devoran Pilot Gig Club's first Cornish Elm gig was called Fear Not and was built by Ralph Bird in his shed adjoining the creek. Results in the water were modest, but as an enthusiastic membership developed, a second gig, Falcon, was commissioned and subsidised by Lord Falmouth. It was built by Bird's former apprentice, Andrew Nancarrow, at his workshop in the Bissoe Valley.

By this time, Devoran PGC had cemented its reputation as a friendly, hospitable club that gave its all on the water but maximised the social opportunities that gig rowing could offer.

As in other sports, the rapid transfer of allegiance between local teams can occur and for a few years in the early 1990s Devoran gained the membership of a group of successful, ambitious rowers due to a fall out with their former clubs over team selection. As a consequence, for a year the men's A crew made the final of both the World and County rowing championships, a notable achievement for any club.

But then this elite crew broke up through retirement or the desire to move on to new challenges elsewhere. The club quickly reverted to its former status, less fanatical of ambition and generally more laid back on, and particularly off, the water.

The rowing strength now seemed to reside with the women, a more focused and considerably more sober bunch than the men. In recent years, two World Championship finishes within the top 25 boats (out of

80 to 90 entries) indicated a dedication to training and a competitive desire.

One year, the majority of the women's crew even agreed to give up drinking between New Year and the start of the Isles of Scilly World Championships at the beginning of May. However, this did cause a certain degree of controversy among crew members as one or two continued drinking modestly in public while others were suspected of furtive binges... the empty bottles of wine left out for the dustman were duly noted!

Before the May World Championships the men always talked a good race, predicting top 30 finishes and an improvement on the sorry capitulation of the year before. But our A team rarely finished within the top 45 crews and the B crew were just relieved to finish at all.

Points of Interest

An article from The Graphic, *in 1887 describes a gig race with a difference; "this season a gentleman suggested that two crews might be found to row the seagoing six-oared pilot gigs off the Port of St Mawes, one to be composed of Old Boys and the other to be Young Boys whose united ages were to show a remarkable disparity. The figure suggested was 500 years, and the two crews were selected and matched who turned out to be strong and able boatmen and by no means unworthy competitors. The united ages of the young crew totalled 79 while the veterans reached the wonderful aggregate of 580, two of 90 years each.*

"Some hours before the time of the race a steamer, having on board the mayor and cooperation and a large number of gentlemen from the City of Truro, steamed up the

harbour and expressed a desire to see the special race. As they could not wait until the official time appointed, the crews consented to oblige with a preliminary contest and a good round was marked off.

"At the firing of a gun, the youngsters dashed off and managed to round the first mark about a length ahead, but on coming up the straight the Old Boy's, steadied down to a long powerful stroke, soon collared them, then drew ahead and were never caught again. The visitors were astonished by the rowing powers displayed by the veterans and the bow oarsman, 90 years old, came on board and thankfully received an extra prize. This old salt explained he had never rowed or sailed in a regatta before, but that he was resolved to turn his attention in that direction, and accepted an invitation to join in a contest at a subsequent date.

"A subsequent race was also won by the veterans by a good lead. This was a gamely rowed contest and Mr J C Kenerley, JP, who had witnessed it from his yacht, invited the old boys and young boys to take tea, an invitation to which they cheerfully responded. The old men, by their lively wit and robust health, made it difficult to believe that they were on the shady side of life before the jubilee period we had celebrated had commenced. When told their exploits would appear in The Graphic *they said it would be something to talk about when they were old".*

Chapter 4

Training on Kippers and Guinness

The gig racing season finally ends in September, the Great Thames River Race, being sandwiched between the Men's and Women's County Championship weekends at Newquay. The World Championships have been decided in early May and the Tribute Challenge has been won or lost during the three starred events from June through to the end of August.

The pecking order has been finalised; April's dreams and aspirations hardened into raw data. The once fresh paint is now chipped and peeling off the wood of boats as battered and knackered as their crew members.

It's now time to take stock of and evaluate another long season. To ask some hard questions:

Did we meet our goals?

Did we have any goals?

Are we satisfied with what we've achieved?

How do we prepare for next season and move the club forward?

The answer to this last question is rarely straightforward. In common with other gig clubs we have a hugely diverse membership, individuals with many and varied reasons for their involvement in the sport, a wide range of different motivations and aspirations.

For example, there are the older members, the

predominantly over 50s, who are still going through the motions, just doing what they have done for decades and rowing and singing and drinking the summer months away. Their prime motivation is to continue to take part, to do it while they still can, to be gig rowers until the effort and pain finally bring a cherished, unique way of life to an end.

For some, racing, competing, is still in their blood. The spirit still burns strongly despite the outward signs of physical decline. The rowing stroke slows, the waistline increases, the hair follicles decrease and the muscles soften.

Then there are the younger, ambitious members. The twenty and thirty somethings who want their sweat and toil to amount to more than 50th place in the championships. This is now their sport, their chance to pit themselves against the best and come out on top. A chance to strut their stuff on the waves.

Between these two groups are predominantly social members. The novice women who seek gentle sea air and a little light exercise. Not for them to row through blistered raw hands or train in lashing rain into mountainous seas. This is their equivalent of a Hampstead Gym on Water, the fire and fury of racing is another world.

Finally, the men whose priority is to use rowing as purely a means of generating an unquenchable thirst. Men who aspire to drink a pint for every stroke they pull in the water and will have forgotten their place in the race well before last orders.

In the past there has been no doubt where Devoran fell on the ultra competitive – primarily social continuum. We didn't call the 'Old Quay Inn', our local pub, 'the Office' for nothing. Devoran could out-drink, out-sing and out-party the opposition from Land's End to Weymouth but on the water it was a different story. Although rarely last we were certainly more used to seeing the sterns rather than the bows of other boats. In short, we were minnows on the water but great Whites in the bar. According to local opinion a "drinking club with a rowing problem".

Technique was not a word overused at the Devoran club, the word invoking nearly as much panic and apprehension as the landlord's call for "last orders".

As for the pursuit of technical excellence…

Some of coaching methods hadn't progressed too much past the "yes that's it, pick up the pointed end and put the spade shaped blue bit in the water. Now pull like ****!" Not that everyone did not have their own style, they did (more inadvertent than conscious), but no two people seemed to do it in the same way. Now, I'm a great fan of individualism in sport, your Wayne Rooneys and Jason Robinsons. I'd always pay to watch them, but even with my limited experience I'm not sure that rowing is the right sport to encourage it. I once heard a spectator watching a Devoran men's team remark:

"God, that one in the middle is a great rower isn't he, so much quicker than the rest and what a spectacular backlift".

I passed this on to the rower in question who beamed with pride.

It reminded me of one of my standard replies at interviews when asked if I was good at group work, "Yes bloody right I am, but those other unco-operative bastards don't have a clue".

The beauty from our members' perspective was that you can drink and row. I don't mean simultaneously, more that a beer gut is not impossible to accommodate in a boat. For one thing, you are sat down and when stationary the oar can rest on it, leaving your hands free to adjust your rollocks or whatever you need to do.

It also provides ballast in rougher water and according to several enthusiastic and bellicose colleagues a 'fuel tank' of readily accessible carbohydrate. Hence the Friday night call to arms to 'carb-up' down the Old Quay. Arsene Wenger eat your heart out, the Doombar bitter is pure liquid pasta and our boys climb into it big time.

To gig row successfully of course serious winter training is essential.

This undeniably apposite statement had about much relevance to our crews as the Koran to the Pope.

To a Devoran gig rower it contained two redundant words, "successfully" and "training".

Our theoretical commitment to hard-core training had an inverse relationship to our alcohol intake.

To give an example, the last time Terry, then our rowing captain, made such a declaration of intent was in the early hours of a recent Sunday morning, while he was in the act of trying to consume a third tumbler of Pernod. I caught something like, "Right from next week, we are all going to get really, really fit".

The slurred orator then fell backwards off his wicker chair, his head rapidly colliding with the fireplace. Colleagues were too far gone to over-react. I heard a mutter of, "Was that his head?" and "****, he knocked my glass over". Bodies were slumped forward like bulls that had been speared by the picadors. Their captain's physical well-being was of less concern than the whereabouts of the last Pernod bottle.

So the predictable end to another evening of club bonding was the cancellation of the following day's training, due to injury, alcohol poisoning and collective apathy.

To return to our end of season predicament. Were we as a club going to continue to accept our lowly position in the rankings as our enduring status quo or were we going to try and change it? The Committee pondered the consequences of taking no action in the longer term... the younger, 'hungrier' rowers would drift off, some attracted by more ambitious clubs and as the older rowers inevitably began to fall away the club would begin to die. In short, gig clubs need a degree of youth, energy and ambition to regenerate.

Handing the reins over to the youngsters would seem the obvious answer but recent experience suggested that a fickleness of commitment can sabotage the best laid plans. For example, a new girlfriend or perfect surfing conditions can soon derail the weekend's gig racing commitment. And then there's the dreaded boat maintenance, the necessity to strip and repaint the boats during the winter months. Hours upon hours of work crawling and scraping on hands and knees during dark, cold November evenings in a draughty cow shed. Immediately half the club members suddenly acquire the work and social commitments of cabinet ministers or find the compassion to visit friends or ill relatives five nights a week. The younger members become as elusive as Osama Bin Laden and his inner circle, resurfacing only when rumour has it that the job is done.

On Saturdays the boat needs to be delivered and

unloaded hours before the racing and afterwards at the end of the day it's going to require ten plus team members to put it away. Pointing this out is not a fertile recruiting strategy with the young.

The problem arises that those who give up their evenings and more of their weekends to maintain the boat and to keep the club running don't always see the need to hand over their place in the boat to the more talented but feckless. They feel they have earned their row.

So was it possible that the way forward could involve a compromise? A strong, committed A crew, comprising the younger members, co-existing in harmony with a more 'relaxed' B crew of older and more socially inclined rowers. A good plan but hard to pull off.

These thoughts were crystallised during the mid-October emergency meeting of all club members. This had been called due to the threat by a tranche of more ambitious rowers to take their talents elsewhere unless something radically changed.

The call was for coaching, early selection of crews for the May World Championships and a training plan for the winter. The bucks were dusting off their antlers and demanding action.

The outcome? Terry, our captain, agreed to arrange for a respected coach from a leading club to commit their time to a Sunday training session in November. Finally we were to be shown the real way, the path to redemption, the road to self-regard.

When the appointed Sunday arrived, conditions on the Carrick Roads were mercifully calm with just a slight on-shore breeze. Martin was already on the quay when the majority of us arrived. A tall, imposing figure in full waterproof suit, he looked bright-eyed, bushy-tailed and eager to cut to the chase. I looked around at his trainees. The comparison did not bode well, surrounded as I was by vacant expressions, bleary eyes and tousled hair. This was Sunday morning and it wasn't only the ex-miners who knew how to let their hair down on a Saturday night.

The session was to consist of going out in four crews, pre-selected by the captain. Martin would stand in the bow each time and record with a video camera our initial efforts, our current rowing style. He would then provide intensive instruction and cox us while we were being videoed again by a colleague in a separate boat. This boat would regularly change positions enabling front and side angles to be obtained.

Our crew was first on, and as I climbed in to take my place at '5' (second from the cox on bow-side) I tripped over the first seat and crashed into the bottom of the boat. Martin's face gave an enigmatic twitch while I put up with the usual sympathetic comments from fellow rowers...

"I see, still pissed from last night... setting a good example... " As I pulled myself up and adjusted the foot stretcher I realised that I had somehow forgotten everything I ever felt I knew about this most technically demanding of sports. Do I twist to the left or the right? How far should I drop my shoulder? How do I position my hands to feather the oar?

Make no mistake, this was going to be an X-rated video (adults only) and not recommended for the faint hearted. The only bit I clearly remember was catching a huge crab as a consequence of having been forcibly moved across the boat to row on my weaker side. Now, to a visiting tourist this might seem a happy outcome, reeling in a large crustacean for future consumption… but in rowing parlance a crab is a total cock-up. The oar having gone in at the wrong angle gets caught in the water and is pulled under the side of the boat. As I tried to push up the oar handle to free it I heard the crack of thole pins and the splintering of wood. A highlight for the camera with sound effects to match!

Seeing a video of yourself rowing is like realising one of these dreams where you suddenly find yourself running naked down Oxford Street past rows of laughing, gesticulating shoppers. There is nowhere to hide and the road goes on forever.

Put simply, the arguments, the prevarications, stop here. Yes, that is you twisting horribly in the boat and lurching forward with the oar with your head nearly down between your legs. It's your oar buried halfway up the shaft and splashing into the water.

Afterwards, as we watch the video in the sailing club lounge, Martin explains that in his experience men generally want to point out the mistakes of others and ignore their own while women are primarily self critical. This would explain why our women crews look technically far superior to the men. They are more inclined to follow the oar in front and maintain a consistent stroke rate. We men think the other five should follow us!

The video rolls on. Eyes down, you pray you're not going to be the first to be singled out, used as a template for technical incompetence.

"Now, you will all notice how Daniel's body is twisting at the wrong angle to the boat, the elbows moving out too much on the catch".

Oh God, ten years of merely compounding bad habits.

Martin embarked on a forensic examination of our lack of technique. This even involved impressive diagrams on a flip chart explaining the relationship of forces to body angles and weight movement. Unfortunately, I never understood physics at school, particularly the bits about fulcrums and levers, and it made even less sense now. (I do remember something about a guy trying to prise the world from its base but I forget the significance). Martin then raised issues such as boat maintenance (rubbing a boat down and drying it out can considerably reduce its weight); crew balance (it's no good having three 16 stone lardies one side and three bean poles the other); fitness and training (this is a hard, aerobic sport and requires stamina as well as technique).

Compliant nodding from the audience, so far so good. But then the bombshell. Martin brought up the subject of alcohol. In fact, he took it head on by suggesting that we would all greatly improve our rowing performance if we didn't immediately follow every rowing practice with a trip to 'the Office'.

Much choking and spluttering into Doombar from shocked audience. This was like suggesting to the Pope that the world would be a better place without an irrational belief in God.

The justifications for such essential team bonding behaviour were immediate and fervent. One member, hand trembling and florid of face, exclaimed loudly that alcohol was merely carbohydrate and therefore could only enhance your performance. As long as you rehydrated your body you were fine. As Brian was a lifelong smoker as well, I was now waiting for a passionate defence of the weed along the lines of how all that sucking and blowing exercised your lungs, kept your fingers supple etc.

At this point John, our own resident doctor, spoke out to support Martin's view, explaining the debilitating effects of our favourite tipple and backing this up with reference to a huge weight of research to be found almost weekly in *The Lancet*. End of argument, conclusion of debate?

Nope, twenty years of research were described as "bollocks" by Brian. Martin must have felt like Galileo in front of the Inquisition, "the sun's going around the earth because it suits us that way so take your fancy theories back to Pisa, pal!"

Anyway, as Keith said in slightly more conciliatory tone, aside from the physical effects, "how could you row if you were permanently miserable, or bond with colleagues over a grapefruit juice?"

Well, as Martin said, it ultimately comes down to what your goals as rowers are and whether you are prepared to make any sacrifices to achieve them. He then scanned every assembled member and asked us directly:

"What does this sport mean to you?"

"How much do you want it?"

Everyone's eyes diverted to the floor and even the glasses stayed untouched for what seemed like an eternity before Colin's voice cut through the uneasy silence.

"Tell me Martin, how many hours a week do you train in the boat?"

As Martin downed the rest of his water, Brian

muttered to no-one in particular, "fish piss in that stuff, boyyo".

"We train every day except Monday. Early mornings, evenings, weekends. An hour at a time, fine tuning our technique, concentrating on style and detail".

I was really impressed with Martin giving up a day of his free time to help us however futile it might prove to be. To get cold and wet and show endless patience and not to laugh or cry or shout or scream. Now we're armed with the knowledge and knowledge is power. So move over Caradon, the Scillies are only 142 days away and we're ready to set our goals.

But realistically, can and will we ever aspire to reach the top of the tree, to be the best? On the way home Brian expanded on his own views:

"We can't become one of those few weird clubs whose members behave like some strange Amish religious sect. The brown rice and pasta brigade who train daily for hours on end and then abuse public houses with orders for crushed fruit juice and non-alcoholic beer; competition for places, ergo times. Dan, it's real third rock from the sun stuff. These are people who go for a run to warm up before the race even starts. It's frightening".

And then Brian spluttered, "They win their races and celebrate on the fizzy water as if it's a surprise, a stunning achievement. Excuse me, but would you expect to lose a Gregorian chanting competition to a closed order of Cistercian monks? Well, it's the same difference isn't it?"

As we are forced to listen to Brian going off on one of his familiar rants, some of us are giving genuine consideration as to where we might want to go, what we could aim to achieve in the year ahead. Has Martin given us the impetus, set us on the road to a more focused and successful season or will the status-quo prevail? Only time will tell

Adapting to a new rowing style after one training session is fraught with difficulties. Patterns of sequenced motor movement acquired over a decade are not so easily changed. How many evolutionary generations do we think it took for our ancestral primates to get off their knuckles and get to the homo-erectus stage? To continue this analogy, watching our rowers from the bow on our second 'independent' practice on Sunday I think we were approaching the Cro-magnon man stage, light years away from even the early Stone Age period. One problem was that everyone seemed to have a slightly different interpretation and memory of what Martin had actually said. Did we really need to lean right back and what exactly was that bit about the angle of the elbow?

The only one constant was the pain. Each row seemed to reduce the stomach to a quivering jelly. The Devoran comfort zone was being put on hold and getting through this was going to take more than the usual increase in Ibuprofen tablets.

A radical thought was being aired as hunched, grimy bodies put the boat away. The gym could be the answer. The muscles needed to be strengthened and trying to hold your stomach in occasionally while queuing at the bar just wasn't good enough.

Now, I had got a bit cynical about gym work and circuit training. On a Friday or Saturday night there is a certain type of person who is always found advocating regular gym attendance. The more pints they down it seems the harder the regime is going to be. It reminds me of men who enthusiastically hold forth at the bar about their sex lives prior to finding themselves with just the landlady for company as the self-effacing couples they've been spouting at have drifted quietly off to get on with the real thing.

Perhaps a few sit ups at home would be a start but there's so little time in the morning, or the kids fall over you in the front room as the dog slobbers across your face.

We all agreed, after Christmas a serious fitness regime would be implemented (although following the festivities it might take a month to get back to the state we were in now).

In the meantime, more pressing social events beckoned such as our Kippers and Guinness morning and a Boxing Day row to the Pandora Inn.

Kippers and Guinness is a Devoran tradition, planned for the first available high tide to Christmas Day. Basically our brisk and brief early morning row is followed by kippers and Guinness back in the Old Quay Inn.

For some this involves a quick half, Christmas greetings and a quick exit to prepare to utilise the rest of the day. For others of us it's party time until the fat lady sings – or comes to throw you out of the bar.

A year or so ago it had snowed overnight prior to our Boxing Day row. Each boatload of returning rowers was greeted by a sky-darkening trail of snowballs, the weight of which almost sunk the boat. A great morning, a great tradition and another good reason to be a Devoran PGC member.

Points of Interest
The language of the Devoran coxswain

Away together – *Leaning forward, everyone rows, starting their stroke at the same time as the person in front.*

Stand by – *In a race situation, the six rowers are prepared to row away together when the starter drops the flag.*

One up together – *Asking for a short, quick stroke to keep the gig on the start-line.*

Back up – *reversing the gig, rowing the oars the opposite way.*

Stroke-side – *stroke-side rowers have their oars to their left.*

Bow-side – *bow-side rowers have their oars to their right – you may be asked to back up bow/stroke-side.*

Ease the oar – *stop rowing.*

After 2, up for 10 – *the cox is asking for more weight, following a build up of 2 strokes, the counting occurs at the end of the stroke.*

Long and strong – *encouraging the rowers to use a long stroke by leaning as far forward and back as possible.*

Big swirls – *a call for maximum power on the stroke resulting in more water coming off the blade of the oar.*

Use your legs – *reminding the rowers to push hard on the stretchers with their legs.*

Give water – *asking other coxswains to give way in a race to avoid a collision.*

Get them in, Dan – *a request that Dan get out of the boat as fast as possible, run up to the bar and order seven pints.*

Chapter 5

It Shouldn't Happen to a Dog

The second Sunday in January and I wake up feeling more toxic than a Ukrainian Nuclear Reactor. New Year's resolutions have long disappeared in a huge fry-up and an extended hair of the dog session. I lie back on the pillow, listening to the loud rattling of hailstones on tiles and glass. I glance at the alarm clock. ****, in 45 minutes I'm supposed to be down at the Old Quay for the first training session of the year. Pull duvet over head... why didn't I stay in last night and watch that film? I'm sure going to the pub again must have been Anne's idea.

A quick wash and a pint of orange juice later and I'm trying to help Anne drag Fern out into the deluge to "be a good girl". The Dachshund's body language says it all... cowering and whimpering by the door, tail firmly jammed between quivering thighs. Her back legs are leaving skid marks across the carpet. Claire, my teenage daughter, glances over and questions our sanity.

"You're mad going out in that. And leave the dog alone, she wants to get back under her sheepskin".

As I look for my coat, I'm finding it hard to breathe. My tracksuit bottoms are cutting into my waist like cheesewire. I consider if they've shrunk in the wash but then glance down at the bulging flesh either side of the elastic. Reality dawns as pregnancy has to be discounted. I enquire if Anne's ready. Receive muttered reply along the lines of, "this will create two more loads of soaking kit and I've already got three loads of washing to do".

"Glad to hear you're so up for it", I remark, pulling my boots over smelly, grey walking socks.

By the time we get down to the quay we're completely soaked. Cheap rowing coats aren't made to resist a deluge of biblical proportions.

As we approach the boat I'm impressed to see Terry setting a good example. Along with one or two other rowers our captain is pulling the cover off Falcon and beginning to unload the oars.

A few muttered greetings. The intensity of the rain makes conversation difficult. We haul the trailer down to the water's edge. Brake on, put the legs down and heave it off the trailer.

I catch Terry's voice. "Have you got the weight?"

A friction squeal followed by a dull thud as the bow slams down on the rocks.

"For Christ's sake," Terry responds. "Do you want a boat for the Scillies or a pile of splintered planks?"

I mentally check to see if there are enough bodies for a crew. Half the regulars haven't turned up. Are they cowering like Fern beneath their sheepskins or has that long awaited OBE for Service to the Community been confirmed, thereby necessitating a Sunday morning attendance at the Royal Garden party? No explanations are forthcoming as Terry's mobile remains predictably silent.

I enquire about the crews. At this point Terry wishes us well before announcing that he is now going home to stoke up the fire and pour himself a large port. "It's this cold and 'flu thing, been suffering all week, just can't shake it off. The only chance is to get warm and dry and try and dose it down with alcohol. Have a good one and be careful putting the boat away".

We ease our bodies on to soaking seats. I feel apprehensive at the prospect of resuming such intense exercise. As the oars drive the boat into the rain, Nikki, our cox, starts a tirade of instructions.

"Hands first, body follows, lean back, push with the legs, elbows in, arms straight". Six directives in the first minute and my corpulent brain has gone into meltdown. A big, red light should be flashing on the top of my head, a warning for information overload. It's hard to breathe into the wind. Under the ferocity of the hailstorm, my face stings as if handfuls of gravel were being thrown at it by sadistic children. The oar keeps bouncing out of the thole pin.

Eventually we return to the shore. A few people are huddling together like Emperor penguins on an ice floe. I notice Adam shivering. As usual he isn't wearing a coat. What is it about teenagers and coats and common sense?

Jason leaves the huddle by announcing that he "has to go and play squash". This makes a lot of sense as he has just come down to rowing, an activity requiring a very different shaped implement! Nikki enquiries if anyone else wants or could row again. Rapid turning of backs and barrage of excuses involving child transport; granny coming for lunch; a hospital visit. So democracy rules and the boat is bundled rapidly away without dissent.

Claire looks up as we walk in through the door

"Feel better for that, do we Dad? Oh, I'm so envious of your hobbies… just to think I might have been out there".

Claire's face turns back to the television, a second repeat of Eastenders. Fern just groans and rolls nearer the fire.

Chapter 6
Lycra and the Perils of the Internet

The effort of adopting the new, hold-back at the end of the stroke style, had led to the women's crews and the men's A crew feeling fitter and more confident and the men's B crew... experiencing chronic back pain. The tell-tale signs were there... shoelaces left undone, an inability to reverse the car, gardening delegated to wives. (In comparison to my posture, the Hunchback of Notre Dame would have looked like the founder of the Alexander Technique.)

Discussion on the beach centred around the relative merits of local physios and chiropractors. Ibuprofen and Voltarol were circulating like sweets.

As I said, the A crew, younger and more supple, seemed to be faring all right and looked all set for the Scillies. But then there was the problem of Brian.

Brian, recently divorced, had decided to search for suitable mates through internet dating and, not to put too fine a point on it, seemed to be hitting the jackpot. Numerous and exotic examples of the fair sex appeared in the pub to be introduced to incredulous team-mates.

According to Brian what they all had in common was an unbridled enthusiasm and energy for the more physical side of life. Crew mates listened attentively to Brian's description of each new encounter.

"Christ," commented Jezza as Brian departed home with what looked like a Russian lap-dancer, "he's found Shangri-La hasn't he, the dirty bastard, a shag-fest with an ever willing and varied cast".

But then something strange started happening to Brian. His increasingly gaunt face confirmed a noticeable weight loss and his drinking started to spiral out of control. His walking was becoming laboured and he made plaintive reference to back pain. A rash had spread across his body. He was regularly seen in the bar frantically scratching at his groin.

One night he took me aside. Brian needed us to understand that his lifestyle was beginning to depress him. He talked about the need for a stable relationship, companionship, empathy. Casual sex was no longer satisfying without commitment. I'm ashamed now to admit my first response was flippant and along the lines of "Oh yeah Brian, what a terrible burden to bear, having to try and satisfy half the female population of Cornwall. But you know, however terrible it is, someone's got to do it and Lady Luck chose you… "

Then I realised my terrible mistake. This man was not amused by my prattling and really did need help.

I tried again…

Happily the situation began to resolve itself when one of Brian's more stable ladies decided to return for a second, and even a third, visit and a proper 'relationship' began to ensue.

Brian's cheeks started to fill out again, the spring came back into his step, his back pain resolved, the rash receded and, most importantly, we once again had an enthusiastic and committed middle of the boat rower!

For the men's B crew, physical preparation for the

Scillies consisted of a handful of parties culminating in a final weekend of team bonding. The usual format, a pub crawl from 7.00pm on the Friday and a club night at the Old Quay Inn on the Saturday. A barbeque queued for in the rain was followed by much drinking and Cornish singing. Terry made a pre-Scillies speech, not Henry V (for those of you who row this day will forever be proud...) but from the heart, words about club spirit, giving our best and most of all having a bloody good time.

The first entertainment centred around Jerry, one of the younger and fitter members of the A crew, who had secured a contract with a local clothing manufacturer to provide a set of skin-tight, siren-blue Lycra tops. These were to be unveiled to kick off the evening festivities.

As is the Devoran way, everyone was going to be asked to model one. The format was to change in the loo before parading down the 'cat-walk'. Now this style may have flattered Jerry, with broad shoulders and a six-pack, but Lycra is very unforgiving to your average physique. So much hilarity as the fat, the thin, the well-endowed and the pigeon chested strutted their stuff (preserving your personal dignity is not a trait in any way acceptable to the Devoran hierarchy).

The best turn was provided by Terry. His shirt stretched only to about his nipples, leaving the rest of his hairy torso exposed. Terry did a twirl and milked the applause, his laughter setting the tone for the rest of the evening.

A few of the male volunteers then hatched plans to get the attractive and well-endowed landlady to take her turn in the one-size-fits-all Lycra. They initially encouraged other non-members in the pub to have a go before pleading with Jenny. As this didn't work the name chanting approach was tried, an incessant repetition of, "Jenny, Jenny, Jenny".

Unfortunately, at this point the landlady disappeared from the bar area and did not return until the shirt entertainment had been exhausted and the collective focus had moved on.

As the night wore on, more improbable rowing plans were made. At around midnight I proposed that next year we should become the first pilot gig club to row to the Isles of Scilly with a crew of over 50 year-olds. By this time all the mature rowers I could find, who were still standing, thought this was a great idea. A rational reaction to the reality of the demands of 12 hours rowing through some of the Atlantic's strongest, and most dangerous currents could wait for another day.

Our new women's B crew, mostly consisting of local art students, were now receiving increasing attention from Brian, still single and our most ardent and, one has to say, our most successful womaniser. This fox in a chicken run scenario was interrupted by Nikki, the women's captain, who pulled Brian aside to point out that she wished her crew of Scillies virgins to remain that way. And anyway, maintaining their physical and psychological health remained her priority. The back-off message was clear.

Several of last year's women's crew, who had fallen pregnant during the winter, had also come to the party. This prompted Terry to say how he appreciated that some members of the club were making an effort to look to the future and produce a junior rowing crew. But, as only four were pregnant and a future crew needed six,

Terry then generously offered his immediate services to any unattached girls who wished to support the future of the club in this way.

I doubt that anyone remembers how the night ended. But rumour has it that Jezza's facial bruising was due to "falling off a high pavement". Martin was found the next morning asleep in the coal shed at the bottom of a neighbour's garden.

Chapter 7

The Isles of Scilly and the World Championships

There is the one stand-out date in the gig rower's calendar. The first bank holiday weekend in May. The World Championships in the Isles of Scilly, the gig rowers' Mecca. This is our Lord's, Aintree, Brands Hatch and Wimbledon rolled into one. Three days of fierce competition on the water and frantic drinking on the land. For a gig rower in spring all roads lead to Hugh Town, the capital of St Mary's. Or they would do if it wasn't cut off from the mainland by twenty-eight miles of Atlantic Ocean!

To set the scene: amid a deafening and raucous clamour, a sea of sweaty bodies fights to establish their supremacy, jostling for position before the bell tolls to end the contest... but let's move on from a description of Friday night in The Bishop and Wolf.

Imagine the sight of ninety brightly coloured, freshly painted gigs, a latter day Armada, spreading out across the strait between the islands.

Only the sound of the oars driving into the sea and the shrill instructions of the coxswain are audible above the rhythmic clunking of the pins. A magical picture as crews from as far afield as America, the Faroe Islands, France and Holland battle it out with the Cornish (and those from Devon, Dorset and Wales) for the ultimate prize, the World Pilot Gig Championship.

Points of Interest

On account of the important strategic location of the Isles of Scilly, the first Atlantic landfall south west of the Cornish coast, two important services were provided by the locally built six-oared rowing boats known as gigs. They were to transport a local man on board the approaching ships to provide a guide through the treacherous local waters and secondly as rescue boats to go to the aid of the shipwrecks. As a consequence, pilot gigs were developed as fast, tough, seagoing vessels that could get a man onto an incoming ship as quickly as possible and, crucially, before rival boats. These pilots could then steer the ship in through the hazardous currents and rocky outcrops to safe water and thus claim the substantial pilotage fees.

The construction of these high performance rowing boats reflected their intended purpose. The gigs were built out of tough, flexible Cornish Elm with an overlapping plank structure, 'clinker', for greater strength and durability.

Geologically the Isles of Scilly are a collection of large lumps of granite laying twenty-eight miles off the Cornish coast. Sparse in population and almost totally lacking in modern tourist facilities they are one of the wettest, windiest outposts of the British Isles. To get there you have three options. Two are airborne; the helicopter that flies from Penzance, or the eight-seater plane that departs from Land's End 'Airport'. The other route is a torturous experience for even the hardiest of travellers, a three-hour crossing on the Scillonian, a small, flat-bottomed boat nicknamed 'the vomit comet'. Part of me would like to leave it at that, to provide just the bare facts, enough to discourage all but the most pig-headed from visiting. Why? Because I'm selfish enough to want to preserve these unique islands from the corrosive effect of mass tourism so prevalent on the mainland.

The subjective truth is that these lumps of granite form one of the world's most beautiful of archipelagos. Green islands of exotic flowers, medieval field systems and wondrous rock formations necklaced by soft, pure white sand and lapped by the clearest, turquoise sea. Small communities of timeless charm, seemingly unsullied by the arcades, nightclubs and mass entertainment so essential to the modern world. At the time of writing St Mary's doesn't even have a cinema. The attraction here is the sea, the sky and the landscape. When the locals get excited at seeing a rare bird we are more likely to be talking about a spotted Greenshank than Jennifer Lopez. In this part of the world when enthusiastic reference is made to a 'shag', the subject matter is more likely to refer to a tufty headed black seabird than a spontaneous leg trembler behind the Dog and Duck. So if your idea of a good holiday is a bargain basement Club 18-30 drunken love-in in Ibiza then St Mary's is probably not going to appeal. (Although 'tis true as I describe the rowing weekend some similarities may become apparent.)

Points of Interest

Aside from the use of gigs for pilotage and rescue services they were of use to the local community for more domestic purpose. Doctors were transported from island to island and in the case of emergencies a volunteer crew might have to be awoken and assembled in the middle of a wild and stormy night.

Gigs were also used to take brides and their wedding parties to churches on neighbouring islands. R H C Gillis quotes details of such an occasion on the morning of August 6th 1929. "... the last wedding party to use the gig the Sussex accompanied a bride dressed in blue silk, with a crinoline hat to match, trimmed with orange blossom. She was Miss Bertha Jenkins who was married to Mr Reg Vickery of Broadclyst, Exeter. All the men wore white heather buttonholes".

To many, the journey from Penzance in Cornwall to St Mary's on the Isles of Scilly is almost as much an integral part of the World Championship weekend as the rowing itself.

For those travelling by boat, the Odyssey starts in the early hours of Friday morning as bleary-eyed club members are picked up at rendezvous points by a hired minibus. They are then driven down to Penzance quay by 8.30am. The Scillonian departs at 9.00am, but luggage has to be packed, tickets checked etc.

At 8.45am, hundreds of burly passengers crowd onto the boat and for most there are only two things on their mind: get in the queue for the bacon butties and get to the bar. I can recall the first time I made this trip seeing the expressions of disdain on some of the more refined, non-rowing passengers as they witnessed this scruffy army walking around at 9.00am with a butty in one hand and a slopping pint in the other. No tea out of china cups for this lot!

On this voyage, I recall looking twice at a middle-aged and smartly dressed man and recognising (I think!) John Redwood, the Conservative politician. He was attired in pressed blazer, grey tailored trousers and shiny black shoes. His female companion was wearing a long, flowery dress. So, self evidently then, not signed up members of the Zennor gig crew.

In some respects, I feel sorry for those innocent holiday makers who inadvertently plan a quiet retreat to the Isles of Scilly during the first weekend in May. Imagine finding your peace disturbed by an army of rowers and supporters who move through the catering facilities of the main islands like rapacious locusts through African crops. No pasty or barrel of beer escapes their attention as the shops, cafes and pubs are laid to waste. (It may surprise you, however, there are those who choose to come this weekend because they like the atmosphere, the buzz and to feel part of a major event... yes, I meant to use that adjective – after all I am in it).

The stars of the journey are the incomparable Falmouth Town Band. They support all Cornish occasions, including the invasions of Twickenham, by marching around in traditional Cornish kilts and playing what Anne describes as a racket. But it's a Cornish racket, and incorporates such enduring classics as 'Going up Camborne Hill, coming down' and of course the Cornish anthem *Trelawney*. (In which if memory serves me correctly thousands of Cornishmen march up and down hills). Always a crowd rouser, this is invariably completed with loud shouts of "OGGY, OGGY, OGGY, OI, OI, OI". (God knows why. I'll ask Terry and get back to you).

So the band serenades the rowers on and off the boat, drums banging. At the time of departure, just after lunch on the Monday, the hundreds of tired, still drunk or hungover crew ascend the gangway to this unique accompaniment. The band then continue to play on the deck as the boat is cast off. Celtic songs are sung and with all the passengers moving to one side the boat lists alarmingly over towards the harbour. A wonderful and moving piece of traditional Cornish theatre.

It takes approximately three hours to cover the forty-odd treacherous miles of Atlantic, between Penzance and St Mary's. There is usually a rolling swell, if not worse, and being of flat-bottomed construction (which is more than can be said for the passengers) the boat lurches around like a homeward bound drunk.

You start off trying to drink a pint and before it gets to your lips it ends up as a half. One word of advice... never stand down wind of green-faced passengers. I learned that the hard way and ended up throwing away an overcoat.

At the end of the return journey, the departing passengers are quite a sight. The after affects of two-and-a-half-days of rowing, a final night out on the juice, a late-into-the-night party, a good few hairs of the dog and figures emerge looking like soldiers from the trenches. Spent warriors, eyes sunken into ashen faces, ready for a timeless sleep. Just don't check the Tuesday morning work attendance figures. Oops, not the thing to say!

The Isles of Scilly Steamship Company sponsor the World Pilot Gig Championships. For a modest fee they transport the gigs and offer club members a reduced fare on the Scillonian crossing and on the Airbus which is also under their ownership.

Without their generosity this annual, glorious, pilgrimage wouldn't happen.

If the boat has a reputation for recycling the

passengers' breakfasts this is not exactly the owners' fault as the lack of a deep keel is due to the modest depth of the water in St Mary's harbour. Many love the journey, the smell of the open ocean, the beautiful vistas, passing dolphins... Personally I'd rather have my teeth removed with rusty pliers.

So I avail myself of the company's other mode of transport and fly. This is an interesting experience in itself. The airport near Land's End consists of two corrugated iron sheds in the middle of what appears to be a large farm. The first time I flew I recall praying that they would remember to remove the cows from the runway. The planes are the size of family saloon cars (albeit with wings) and the proximity to your seven fellow passengers is intimate.

You may feel vulnerable taking off and landing in such a noisy and lightweight plane, but with a 100 per cent safety record, promptly adhered to take-off times and a guaranteed fifteen to twenty minute journey it has always seemed to me to be the sensible way to travel.

Chapter 8
A Scillies Virgin

This unique weekend is about competition on the water and camaraderie off it. The local reputation of a prolonged booze-up is hard on those committed competitors whose three months of hard training is concentrated into the four main races. OK, millions of pints are sunk and apparently the weekend sustains the entire economy of the islands (I forget the exact figure, something like ten pints for every stroke pulled) but supporters now arrive in their thousands and their agenda is less focused on bird-watching and island-hopping than elbowing their way to the bar and "getting them in".

The World Championship format consists of four races, two on Saturday, the first around lunchtime, the second in the early evening, and a repeat of this schedule on Sunday. The first race is the longest... a free-for-all from the island of St Agnes back to the harbour on St Mary's, a distance of approximately three miles. The position the boats finish in this race determines the order for the next races. These are rowed in heats of twelve from Nut Rock off the island of Sampson back to St Mary's harbour. This is a shorter race of a mile-and-a-quarter. The first and last three boats are then promoted and demoted after each heat. The advantage of this arrangement is that all crews take part in all the races and by the last heat they should have established their correct competitive level. The weaker crews are set off first. The last twelve boats making up heat A are the last to leave Nut rock for the final race to St Mary's to establish a champion.

Competitors and supporters generally make a long weekend of it as racing also takes place on Friday evening. The veterans race at around 6.30pm is followed by The Plate race, originally a Truro/Scillies challenge race, but now very much used as a warm-up for the main weekend event and an opportunity to give club members not competing in the main championship a row. This is the end of April, the first weekend in May, so the weather is at its most unpredictable. I have rowed in flat calm water in temperatures over 20°C and into the teeth of a force seven gale. I learned an early lesson never to complain about the conditions. This is sea rowing and the sea in front of you is the only one that's available! All conditions pose a different challenge and it's the same for everyone... so pick up your oar my son, think positive and never whinge.

They say just as with your first relationship you always have a special memory of your first Isles of Scilly Championship. The analogy of losing your virginity fits well... the sense of terrified anticipation and excitement; the fumbling and technical incompetence; poor timing; the thrill of the finish, the subsequent deep relaxation and post-event bonding in the bar.

My first World Championship was my first-ever gig race. I didn't know what to expect. All I had to go on were the tales of the more experienced rowers. Tales of the fierce cross-currents, the boat clashes, the legendary crews, the beauty of the evening light.

My memories of that first championship in 1995 remain vivid. Trying to eat breakfast but being too nervous to chew it; the build-up throughout the morning as the first race approached; preparing the boat on the green in front of the beach; the sight of dozens of other brightly painted gigs, their crews quietly adjusting their seats; choosing strong pins; muted conversation; a dry throat; compulsive time checking, willing the race to start. Desperate, in fact, to get on the water to start to row, to concentrate on one simple action, to cut through the tension. At last one thirty. The women crews stagger knackered from the boat. We take their oars and congratulate them on their efforts. We pull the gig up onto the beach, fetch our own oars, adjust the stretchers, check the pins and the seats. Trainers are thrown into the boat and we push her off. Soon we are leaving the harbour, joining a posse of other boats heading out across to the far island of St Agnes. For the first time it dawns on me, as I look out towards this distant landmass. We were actually going to have to row out there just to come back in! To row the race course once before turning straight around and rowing it again.

Having had little time to train and lacking all but the most rudimentary technique I was getting completely knackered well before we got near St Agnes. It then crossed my mind that I may not even get to the start-line, the first competitor ever to collapse on the way out... ! I tried to banish such negative thoughts and just concentrate on each stroke... watch the oar in front, in and out together, try and lean back.

An amazing scene comes into view for spectators looking towards St Agnes rocks... between fifty and one hundred colourful gigs floating around, waiting for the stragglers. Two start boats were now in position, one with the flag, an imaginary line running between them. A long line of gigs started to fan out; it was a case of find your gap and hold your ground. Some banter within and between boats – a voice came across to us.

"John, are you still doing this you senile old goat?"

"Keith, you bastard, there's less miles on my clock than your's, you're probably older than my mother!"

Some crews silent, breathing heavily, concentrating.

The voice of our cox, Pat, cuts through, "right boys the flag's up; concentrate, oars forward just above the water; deeps breaths; let's think about it; just listen to me; eyes down the boat, it's dropping any second".

The umpire's voice interrupts, "back up Falcon, back up Royal".

The tension builds again.

"Royal back up now or you'll be disqualified".

Pat's voice again. "Get ready... GO! Three strokes off the arms, building for six, take the stroke rate up, maximum power".

My hands jar as my stroke is interrupted by a clash with an oar from another boat. I hear their cox, "steer clear Royal, give us water!"

More clashes... cursing from our boat as their cox glares across.

"For **** sake, move over, give water!"

And then we're free again, veering off into clear water. Oars splashing, shouting and boats everywhere.

Pat's in the groove. "Right, now I want ten big ones... building for two... I need them now, on one, on two, now let's go... a one, a two, three, strain every sinew, oar to the body, ram arms forward, remember to push with those legs. That's doing it boys... pulling alongside Locavar... "

I see the strain on their faces, their cox leaning forward and back, forward and back. Pat's voice again, "come on, don't let her drop. Keep on the weight. This is when we need it. Grit your teeth, pull it to me... drive her on... good boy Dan, that's it keep ripping it through the water".

An adrenaline fuelled blur... time has no reference point... minutes or hours pass... aware of more clashes along the way... shouts and oaths... duels with other boats. Races within a race. We pass some, more pass us and then the hooter and the cox's instruction to stop rowing, ease the oar. "Well done boys great effort".

I lean over my oar, gulping for breath and spit into the sea. The last boats are pulling in behind us; the first crews are nearly back on the beach.

"Three cheers for Locavar", our nearest rival... I can barely raise a grunt.

A memory of lying on the rocks near the beach, shaking fingers scrabbling the wrapping off a Mars bar. Desperate for that quick intake of sugar. I lay back on the rock and tried to close my eyes to recall the race. A wave of relief, quiet satisfaction. My first gig race over. The championships under way and I was no longer a Scillies virgin!

Points of Interest

Two thousand and five marked the 16th consecutive year that the Isles of Scilly have hosted the World Gig Championships.

The local paper, The Cornishman, *called the decision to dream up the World Championships "the ultra secretive project X" that finally came to fruition in May 1989.*

Initially the number of gigs competing was in single

figures. The recent growth in the number of entries has been truly staggering.

For the past decade gig rowing has been spreading further and further afield and clubs have now been established in such diverse locations as Boston, USA, France, the Faroe Islands and Holland.

The most recent new recruits are Porthgain Rowing Club in Pembrokeshire who commissioned Ralph Bird of Devoran to build their gig, Kathrin Rose. At least they are unlikely to lose their oars as they are emblazoned with the image of the Welsh flag.

The current men's champions are the Caradon Club from Saltash, who have achieved a remarkable nine wins in ten years. Falmouth have dominated the women's event, the Isles of Scilly crew being their only close challenger in recent years.

I was soon to learn from experience that how people apply themselves to the mental and physical challenge of rowing the World Championships would vary considerably. George, one of my first fellow crew members, could be seen leaving the bar minutes before a race chewing a huge Cornish pasty. He would get in the boat and continue to eat this while rowing the first few hundred yards out of the harbour with the oar in his free hand. Another colleague, Nigel, was swigging from a flask of clear fluid. I had always assumed, understandably, that this was water or a performance enhancing drink of the Red Bull variety.

However, just before we started the St Agnes race, being desperate to wet my lips, I 'borrowed' this bottle and took a large swig. I immediately coughed it up again down the front of my rowing vest. It was what the Red Indians would have called 'fire water'. I later discovered that the main ingredients were vodka and sambuca with a dash of lemonade.

Over the years, I have also discovered that as you row out from the beach everyone has their own way of preparing psychologically for the race ahead. Some row in quiet contemplation, mentally preparing themselves for the supreme effort to come. Others like myself expel their nervous energy by giving a running commentary on the scene around them, from the look of the other crews to 'helpful' tips on ornithology.

Terry, our captain, who sits immediately behind me in the boat, was typically tolerant of my most recent attempt to give an illuminating update on the local bird population;

"For ***** sake Dan will you stop prattling on about the ******* seagulls and let the rest of us concentrate on what we're here for… getting this boat from the start-line back to the beach as fast as possible so we can get to the bar before the rest of these bastards block it up".

"All right Terry, I've got the message". I sulk, before inadvertently blurting out, "Oh my God, look at those magnificent black wing tips, its got to be Gannets… "

I feel an oar handle dig hard into my rib-cage and I refocus my eyes straight ahead.

Points of Interest

One less noble use of the remarkable sea worthiness of the pilot gig was as a smuggling vessel. It is said that one famous oarsman, James Nance, made as many as twenty-five smuggling expeditions to and from the Brittany coast. A journey that could be as long as 250 miles and in rough water take as long as thirty hours.

Eventually the Governor of the islands grounded Nance on St Martin's and in a desperate effort to reduce smuggling confiscated cottages from others that he thought had been bought with illicit earnings.

Battling the elements

As I sat in the Atlantic Hotel on the Saturday night with my fellow rowers we fell to reminiscing about our most memorable races.

The year 2003 will forever be prominent in the memories of all those who rowed in this most dramatic of World Championships.

On the Thursday prior to our departure the weather chart was a threatening portent of what was to come... a jet black depression the size of America screaming in from the Atlantic with isobars closer together than Ikea shoppers at a New Year's sale.

The weathermen threatened metrological Armageddon and for once they were right.

Fortunately, I flew over to the Scillies, leaving my wife to the Friday morning crossing on the Scillonian (well, we had to economise somehow and anyway Anne likes boats). She reported that cutlery and chairs were smashed, passengers thrown across the galley and strong men crawled around the toilets groaning in torment. An average three hour journey took over four-and-a-half hours. I have to say I felt queasy looking down at the conditions from the plane.

Naturally we assumed all rowing would be cancelled on health and safety grounds. But no, Saturday dawned and as the flags on the Green were being ripped off their poles and the boats in the harbour gyrated like Elvis fans the announcement was made that the first race would go ahead. As I went into my colleague Nigel's room to get my kit I caught him swigging deeply from a rum and shrub bottle. "Run out of lemonade have you?" I enquired. To which he replied, "Dan, have you looked outside, only a fool would go out there sober".

He had a point. The wind was blowing a force seven. As I walked down towards the beach I caught Terry's eye. "Terry, I've got young, dependent children at home. It's irresponsible for me to go out there".

Terry's eyes narrowed. "Dan your children have left school. Now pick up that bloody oar and get your head together".

The row out to the start-line was like no other experience I have had before or since. As soon as we left the harbour the waves were so big and the troughs so deep that you couldn't see anything behind or in front of you. Your body was smashed into the side of the boat and the freezing water burst over your back. We climbed one wall of water after another before crashing down into the troughs. One minute the oar was dragging down in the water, the next it was five feet up in the air.

The cox's voice was partially lost in the roar of the sea. "Be strong in the water, take control of the oar. Don't let the sea control you. Keep in time, concentrate, and drive with your legs".

Nigel was then heard screaming, "Oh my God!" as the sky disappeared under another mini-Tsunami. As my life flashed before me, I prayed for absolution before emerging from the other side spitting out water.

Now, I have always admired the Grace Darlings and the Shackletons of history, people who had valiantly stood up against all that nature could throw at them...

but they had a purpose to risking their lives... if I went to the bottom of the ocean my heroics weren't about to be indoctrinated into the next generation of school children. After the 'Irresponsible Idiots Drown off Scillies' type headline, that would be it. Oblivion.

It took another hour to get to the start-line, inching forward into the tide and the winds. Another oar floated past, it was the third we had seen dislodged. I half expected a body to be next... "Oh look, I'm sure that's old George from the gig Locavar. You can tell by the colour of his rowing vest".

Eventually we staggered to the start-line, the last boat. As we turned the boat around the flag went down immediately. We surfed back, thrashing the oars through the huge rollers we had battled against on the epic outward journey. Seventeen minutes of pure exhilaration and we were washed into the harbour, half drowned and hardly capable of crawling up the beach.

What an experience. I'd thoroughly recommend it. Rarely have I felt as alive as when I was battling into that force 7, adrenaline pumping, on the edge. In retrospect I feel privileged to have been a part of it, especially as I lived to tell the tale.

Points of Interest

In the 19th Century and beyond, Cornish Pilot Gigs played a key role in rescuing crew and salvaging cargo from those unfortunate ships that were driven onto the rocks off the Isles of Scilly.

The wreck of the Sciller in 1875 proved one of the most tragic events to be associated with these islands. Although the crew of the gig O and M were able to save five lives, 310 people drowned and it was reported that the island children were kept in their houses to spare them from the trauma of the sight of such a long procession of coffins.

A decade later, December 17th 1885, is also a date of great historical significance for Scillonians. On this day the crew of the gig the Golden Eagle played an heroic part in rescuing sailors from the SS Sussex and salvaging cargo that included bullocks and frozen geese. As the gig historian R H C Gillis has documented, the Golden Eagle went on to acquire a remarkable salvage record, being the first gig at the scene of numerous other local ship wrecks. "In 1898 she was at the wreck of the SS Brinkburn. She was at the wreck of the full rigged ship Erik Rickmers in 1899 and during the same night at the wreck of the French Barque Parame. On April 10th, 1910, she was at the wreck of the SS Minnehaha and for several weeks did salvage work helping to lighten the vessel".

Another heroic date in the 20th Century for Scillonians is 1907 when the Slippen launched from St Agnes was the first gig to the seven-masted schooner, the TW Lawson. Tragically only three of the 19 crew survived but that should not diminish our respect for the efforts that day of the brave Slippen gig crew.

Gig rowers' humour is not always noted for its subtlety. On one Saturday night, halfway through the competition, Jerry, acting as a spokesman for the Devoran A crew, unfurled a hand-printed T-shirt with the pictures of five crew members on the front. The space where the sixth was supposed be was replaced with a question mark. Underneath this was written, "where's the ginger twonk?" and on the back of the

T-shirt was a picture of the missing crew member underlined with the message, "at least your crew love you!" Unbelievably, the shirts were circulated to all the crew with much hilarity, with Adrian, the individual with his portrait on the back, presumably being expected to see the funny side. Admittedly, from an observation of his facial expression and body language, he did appear to take a short period of time to adjust to the crew's collective sense of humour. However, within a few minutes Adrian appeared to be wearing it with pride while his colleagues jeered, cheered and slapped him on the back.

I was relieved to see that an action that would turn a ChildLine spokesman weak at the knees was used as a bonding exercise by this 'band of brothers'. Perhaps it works on the Madonna principle that all attention/ publicity is good... hey, who wants to sit in the corner and be ignored.

Jerry then produced another handwritten T-shirt advertising the 'Dick of the Day'. This was unanimously presented to Judy, an A crew women rower, for peeing twice into a bucket on the start-line and catching two crabs on the way in. On the back, this had written messages such as, "if you think I'm behaving like an idiot ring this number: 878432".

Again, this seemed to be taken in good spirit and worn by Judy with a flourish.

Points of Interest

Myths and legends abound in the Celtic outposts of the far south west and therefore it is not surprising that some are interwoven with the history of Cornish pilot gigs.

One such myth, a well rehearsed story on the Isles of Scilly, explains the derivation for the name of the early 19th century gig, Bonnet. R H C Gillis records this tale in his short book, The Pilot Gigs of Cornwall and the Isles of Scilly.

"This gig was named after an old lady who lived on St Martin's who was supposed to have powers of witchcraft. The name was reputed to give her luck in pilotage. When the Bonnet was on such an errand the old lady would go up the hill and wave her bonnet to give the oarsman power. After her death her son would take the bonnet onto the hill and place it on a gorse bush and say, 'Now Mother, do your best'. There was always a certain taboo on the name Bonnet after the old lady's passing and the gig was always spoken of as 'the old hat'".

Chapter 9

The Bishop and the Pole Dancers

As I have said, the final two races take place on the Sunday, the boats congregating off Sampson, a small uninhabited island a mile north of St Mary's. They are then lined up in groups of twelve by the side of buoys before the starter flag drops.

There are advantages to not being very good... primarily because you get to row back in the first or second race instead of drifting around behind the start-line for hours freezing your proverbials off. You can then get back to the harbour and watch the other boats come in or row back to the beach and beat the rush to the bar!

At the end of the final race the finishing positions are clarified and the closing ceremony takes place on the Green by the side of the gigs. The ceremony is quite long as each group winner is awarded a medal. So with 96 gigs competing there may be eight male and eight female crews on and off the podium before the final fanfare for the eventual winners. *We are the Champions* blares out over the tannoy, red smoke is released and after the presentation of the individual trophies and the cup itself each winning crew member jumps off the fifteen foot high stage into the crowd.

This is an act of great faith in your fellow competitors as the human projectiles may weigh in excess of fifteen stone (and the men considerably more, sorry girls) and take a lot of catching.

By 7.00pm on Sunday the competition is officially over so let the partying begin. This may not have the colour and prestige of the Rio Carnival but for enthusiasm and into the night revelry it comes a close second. The Devoran format is usually a few beers directly after the last row (don't forget we get to the bar before most) followed by a quick rub-down and shower before a rendezvous back at The Bishop and Wolf. Now Devoran may not be the best rowers in the world but we are the party kings. We do the normal Cornish things of singing, drinking and dancing on tables, but there is an inventive streak there as well.

A year or so ago, Terry found a long piece of thick cardboard tubing (God knows where from) and proceeded to drag it into The Bishop. Quizzical expressions as Terry had a word with the landlord. The pole was then secured into the middle of the room as lively, rhythmic music started up. Of course, it's obvious; it was to be an evening of Devoran pole dancing. At about 9.00pm, the first brave volunteers were pushed up to the pole and tentatively swung around it to the clapping of the onlookers.

Others looked on in trepidation as by now Terry had made it quite clear that all Devoran Pilot Gig Club members were to take their turn. As usual, this was non-negotiable participation. By mid-evening the scene had been transformed. Fiona, one of our younger female rowers, was performing erotic simulations up the pole opposite the Scottish barman. He was now stripped down to his underpants, and matching her every move.

The clapping and cheering was deafening and the floor sticky with spilt beer. Apparently I did all right, hanging off the pole and lovingly stroking it before staggering back to my seat to enjoy the exploits of others. I have a hazy recollection that Colin, one of our most senior rowers, was a real hit with the audience; licking the pole all the way down with tongue wriggling enthusiasm while squeezing it hard between his thighs.

I hear a lap dancing club is opening it up in Newquay, so several of us may be contemplating a career move.

On Sunday night you would think that the pubs on the Isles of Scilly would be open until all hours. With thousands of captive rowers with one aim in mind – the partial or complete obliteration of their faculties – the situation is a publican's dream. But no, the islands run a very ordered society, rules are not transgressed and their 10.20pm call for last orders means just that. Now it is true that by this time each man, woman and adolescent is likely to have consumed their own body weight in beer and the poor bar staff are dead on their feet. (To give an example of the Sunday night demand on resources, just one bar in Hugh Town has at any one time as many as 12 staff continuously serving drinks). I've calculated that if all the beer drunk on this Sunday night was poured onto the mainland it would form a lake the size of Lake Michigan in the USA. It's also said that if the barrels were alternatively poured into the sea, the level would rise to such an extent that parts of the Cornish mainland would be instantly flooded.

The second stage of the evening is the barbeque and late-night party. A beach some half-a-mile from the centre of Hugh Town is the centre for this well established and well attended ritual. Thousands of semi-comatose bodies pour out of the pubs and stagger up the hill past the school and down onto the beach. A huge bonfire awaits them plus a stage with live bands and a shed dispensing barbequed food and cans of ale. If sober, watching the rowers move across the sand must be quite comical. Most cover twice the required distance as no one is moving in a straight line. Many seem to mimic the action of newborn foals, seemingly unsure of the connection between their brain messages and leg movement.

The bonfire is huge and it's not unusual to only become really aware of its potency on the Monday morning when one wakes up and looks in the mirror to be shocked by the sight of singed hair and deleted eyebrows! The atmosphere is friendly, even celebratory. The hard graft is over for a week or two and it's time to ease the pain of those blistered hands and sore bottoms with liquid analgesic. However, as you can imagine, given the state of the revellers, incidents can and do happen. One of the younger rowers from a neighbouring club returned from St Mary's with first degree burns across his bottom... Nasty, when you think about it. Apparently he had been up in the dunes with a few mates and they had been having their own barbeque using one of those metal, disposable jobs. After a good few tinnies, they were horsing around having some sort of drunken wrestle, as young men are wont to do, when Adam fell over backwards and landed buttocks first in the charcoal red rectangular container. Eye witnesses report that it was wedged on so tight that he was forced to sprint down the sand and into the sea trailing smoke and giving off a smell like a spit roasting pig. The sound of sizzling when he dived in could be heard right around the beach. Pursed lips and pained expressions all around… well, after we had had a good laugh about it, of course.

To my knowledge, the entire Championship weekend is policed by just two constables. The only violence I can recall hearing about was intra-club. The story goes that the male rowers of a certain South coast gig team had been arguing and feuding all winter about the selection of the A and B crews and everything else besides. It came to a head during this particular weekend and both crews ended up laying into each other with the gusto of feuding cowhands in a B western. Apparently no-one else was involved and it cleared the air in the club.

However, I did once witness a notoriously volatile husband and wife 'team' fall out spectacularly in the Bishop and Wolf, hurling abuse and furniture at each other in equal measure. This culminated in a chair crashing through a window and onto the pavement outside. To see any other couple behaving like this would have been horrific and a definite precursor to their permanent separation; to these two it was a kind of drunken foreplay.

Towards the end of the party (or before that in the dunes) new couples can be seen pairing up. Mutual screaming in the shower is often the next step as rowers inflict jets of hot, stinging water on each other's rubbed-up bottoms. Very erotic; the Marquis De Sade would have approved. Don't knock it until you have tried it.

The Scillonian Club

The haunt of the locals, the authentic St Mary's

experience. Basic décor, offering a basic menu, washed down with real ales at customer friendly prices. I was put off by my first visit. It was early evening and a teenage girl was leaving by the front steps. As I approached the bottom rung she threw up, firing a perfect yellow parabola down the iron railings and across the road. It reminded me of a scene from the Exorcist.

On the last night of the Championships you can hardly squeeze in the door, and as to the prospect of getting to the bar, it was less effort rowing the races. It's hard to describe the density and intensity of the crowd.

Think one of those big days out at Mecca or the opening morning of the Harrods' sale. After more than an hour, one of our club got served and we all shouted our additional orders from the back. So pints of beer got passed across the top of the throng.

By the time mine arrived there was less than half left, the rest having been spilled over the heads of the Roseland crew in front of us. I restrained myself from shouting, "hey mate, that's my beer in your hair. Perhaps you would like to replace it, yeah, and make it snappy".

This is where traditional Celtic singing is orchestrated by that iconic Cornishman Brian Trenoweth.

Standing on a table, this imposing figure conducts the self-appointed choirs through an evening long rendition of old Cornish favourites. This is a sacrosanct Celtic occasion and not a good time for an 'outsider' to start feeding the juke box. So why, year on year, are there only a couple of poor bar staff employed to try and satisfy the thirst of hundreds of gasping rowers?

I have visions of the owners scratching their heads on Monday morning and exclaiming, "blimey, where did that lot come from? Last Sunday there was only two locals and that family from Barnsley".

Now, I know it is an insular place, but there is that banner advertising the World Championships across the main street. The next year I found a solution. I got in early, squeezed in the corner with a coat full of canned lager, so it was "no worries mate" as I soaked up the unique atmosphere and diminishing oxygen supplies without having to risk getting cauliflower ears replicating an English scrummaging practice.

Taking Stock

Tuesday morning 2005, and a pause for reflection;

Did the new style work?

Did the crews improve on last year's places?

For the men's A crew a definite yes to both. Up from 47th to 31st place in 12 months. No threat to the 'big boys' yet, but healthy and encouraging progress, the men's B up from 89th to 85th this time avoiding being in the last heat.

The women's A, a creditable 24th position finish, a few places up on last year and as several key rowers had left to propagate future crew members this was a very good effort.

It's true that the women's B crew, who came 64th, also did well considering they had a virtually virgin crew. For many of them the Scillies had provided their first experience of competitive racing.

So when you eventually get back to the office there is always that first person who bounds up to you with the question, "did you win?"

Well, perhaps I should be flattered that a colleague might consider it possible that I could have been part of a World Championship winning crew… all those hours fine-tuning my body must be paying off. I used to say "No", and leave it at that. But then there is always that goading follow up enquiry, "well, where did you come?" The factual reply would be 85th but hey, why give them the satisfaction. So I merely and correctly state that, "there was a heat below us and we also beat two boats in our own heat". This usually earns an approving nod and suffices, but occasionally there is the Jeremy Paxman questioner who persists "but *where* did you come?"

Then I get narked. "OK pal, so 84 boats may have crossed the line in front of us… but this was the World Championships", or I mutter the number while turning quickly away and marching briskly down the corridor. Competition is getting harder, obsessive even. Where have the amateur days gone, the *esprit de coeur*… ?

Anyway, as I point out to them, if they play a sport, say football or cricket, imagine if they were to be part of the 85th best team in the world at it. Fantastic… wouldn't be so easy to achieve would it? No? Exactly; I rest my case.

Chapter 10
Olympic Advice

You have only to look at the sports pages of the newspapers these days to see that sports psychologists are all the rage. Everyone has to have one: rugby teams, cricket teams, golfers, snooker players and even the local darts team. You know the sort of thing... Positive visualisation I think they call it. Rehearse that perfect conversion, the exquisite cover drive. Imagine that chip over the tree that breaks back to within a foot of the hole, the 160 three dart finish.

The general rule is to close your eyes and recall the feelings you experienced in your body when you once achieved that golden moment. The problem for me with this approach is that it pre-supposes on the one hand that you have had such a moment and on the other hand that you can recall it.

In my earlier days with Truro River Rowing club, the women's captain, a fanatically committed individual, decided that in order to try and gain a marginal advantage on our closest rivals we should enlist the help of 'psychology'. To this end, Frances announced that she had made contact with a sports psychologist who had worked with the British team as they had prepared for the last Olympic Games. Now, although my fellow gig rowers maintained more than a healthy scepticism, this guy did sound the dogs do das... Olympics and all that.

So, one foggy winter evening, Dr Brean did indeed

turn up at our bleak village hall. He was greeted by a spattering of fleece-wearing individuals, with "open minds". I suppose we were expecting someone like that East German guy, Jurgen Grobler, legendary rowing coach and mentor to the great Sir Steve. So Frances's introductory announcement that Brian Brean had been the shrink for the archery team came as something of a surprise. Brian then started his session by confirming that he knew nothing about rowing, and that the only gigs he had heard of involved Wembley and the Rolling Stones. But fear not the oracle continued, have faith my brethren, the principles of psychology are ever transferable.

The suggestions? From the sublime to the ridiculous.

With the aid of a piece of chalk and a temporary blackboard, Dr Brean began to outline the plan. We were to:

1. Beam ourselves down from another planet into the boat (er, why hadn't I thought of that?). This is designed to give a sense of focus and sense of location. Anne said it was so that you "know where you are" – otherwise I suppose you'd sit in the boat and think, "Oh God, where am I now?... er, right". It does ring true in one sense though. I do know quite a few gig rowers from my present club who do appear to have come down from another planet. Unfortunately they always seem to return there after they have rowed! But to be more positive to the good Doctor, an example of the modern utilisation of this technique might be the way the BBC currently introduce us to each football venue in *Match of the Day*... Homing down on to the stadium from a great height to provide an immediate context.

2. We needed to imagine that we were sitting quietly in our boat and doing well in our race. Visualise a positive start, kicking away in front of the other boats; rowing strongly to the first mark; passing other crews; maintaining an optimum rhythm and momentum right to the end. Crossing the line, finishing strongly and in complete control. This could have its merits... But gig rowing in the sea is full of incident and a need for readjustment. Oars bounce out of the pins, pins break and jam in their hole, boats clash and so on... So when challenged by this, Dr Brean added that we had to visualise dealing with such incidents, changing pins, overcoming crabs and moving on after clashes with other crews. All eventualities must have been thought through thoroughly!

3. The third strand of Dr Brean's master plan was the attaching of a card to the back of the rower directly in front of you. On this was to be written, appropriately, the acronym GIG. This was to promote the message 'Get in Gear', meaning focus now on the job in hand. For instance, no idle chatter, concentrate on what needs to be done, practice that visualisation. This seemed logical, but in many respects everyone prepares in their own way (for example there is that colleague who likes to eat a pasty and pass wind in the boat). Also it is not unusual for the race start to be delayed by half-an-hour. This is a long time to be "in the zone". Personally, I have only got the concentration and adrenaline to start focusing when we are called to the start-line, before that I need to stay relaxed!

4. The next activity caused some amusement. All club members were asked to make a list of the factors that for them personally would make their rowing more

effective. These suggestions were then to be placed in rank order. Common themes included; a quality boat, well maintained; regular, well run practice sessions; adherence to a fitness regime. But everyone had failed to grasp that most decisive of factors, *carrot cake*... yes Julie's number one choice! Apparently she cannot row without it. On that first occasion Julie had also considerately brought a large specimen along to help fuel the evening's proceedings. So carrot cake came to figure just below "well maintained kit" in our final list.

5. Finally, Dr Brean's ideas to improve our practice on the water incorporated an interesting new initiative. The Doctor asked for two essentially equal strength crews to be chosen to compete against each other in a race. This was to be a race with a significant difference. Each crew would be told beforehand that they were to be the eventual winners or losers. The important advice, the losers had to push the winners really close, even, if necessary, be prepared to lead the race before backing off at the end. The result, or should I say the psychological interpretation of it, was that the losers felt they had rowed really well on each occasion and could if they had wished have won the race. The conclusion, as the pressure was off them to actually win, they rowed in a more relaxed manner that proved far more effective than the frenetic style of the under pressure nominated winners. An interesting theory, but the Devoran men's B crew don't row encumbered with the pressure or expectation of winning and, well, we don't win. Perhaps we subconsciously slow down to let the other crews through!

So, as a package, did we believe it worked? I could see the logic in some of the advice. Developing mental strength, positive thinking, and rehearsing potential pitfalls. But while gig rowing, like all sports, must have a psychological component, it essentially relies on fitness, stamina, teamwork and, above all, technique. To develop and achieve this requires crews to maximise the time they spend in the boat and in the gym (as opposed to the bar). To my mind, the trouble with visualising your boat's success in the race is that when you inevitably fall behind off the start, because for example of poor timing and then fall further adrift as the course progresses due to inadequate stamina, you end up losing faith in the pre-ordained mental slide show.

Perhaps if the rowing fundamentals are already in place, then trying to home in on the psychological side could create a definite advantage. So if Caradon or Falmouth for example wants to get even better and more dominant, Dr Brean could be your man... or, as I made a few notes, give me a ring and I'll have a go. Expenses in the form of Doombar vouchers please. (And being a life-long fan of carrot cake, I am right there with that idea).

However, my instinct tells me, that I don't think the time is quite right for Devoran PGC to track down Dr Brean. If I suggested it to Terry I think the response might be along the lines of, "Dan, just get the next round in and don't be so bloody daft".

We don't want to complicate life at Devoran PGC. The incentive to finish the race is to get to the bar... That sweet taste of Doombar is reward and motivation enough.

Chapter 11
Cadgwith and meeting Jenny

Points of Interest
Location
South eastern side of the Lizard peninsula.
Famous old fishing cove, that once held the record for the number of pilchards caught in one day. 1.3 million!

Gig Club
Based in the old lifeboat house. First gig, Buller, built by Ralph Bird in 1986. Second boat, Socoa, built in 1990 and named after a French sailing ship that got stranded off Cadgwith in 1907.

The last gig, Rose, was built in 1994 and dedicated to the memory of local fishermen, Tony Colmer and Peter Williams, whose vessel, the Caren Marie, sank off the cove in the same year. Their lives are further commemorated by the 'Tony and Peter' intra-club races.

Cadgwith are very hospitable hosts, but remain very competitive in the water. Great rivals are neighbours Coverack.

Rowing Conditions
Open to the full force of the Atlantic, therefore always a 'roll' and if the wind blows, look out.

Pub Check
A beauty. A traditional local with good beers and a convivial atmosphere. Hosts for the Cadgwith Singers on Friday nights.

Tourist Interest

Unspoilt cove, rugged coastal scenery, authentic smells!, Celebrity watch, quality craft shop, the Cadgwith Cove Inn.

Best Experience

Rowing surrounded by basking sharks.

Cadgwith is a small cove on the Eastern side of the Lizard, that famous granite peninsula which marks England's most westerly point. The simplicity of the few old buildings, the fishing sheds and the huddled thatched cottages pay homage to its roots. Fishing boats are still pulled up on the shingle beach, but these days they are mostly crab and lobster boats as the trawlers out from Newlyn remain the only sustainable offshore commercial fleet.

It's not only fishermen who live here now though. Cadgwith is also the home of some of our best loved thespians. The actress Jenny Agutter (if you're of my generation, you will remember her as the older sister in *The Railway Children*) and James Bolam of *The Likely Lads* fame live there. So a brief stroll around the rugged edge of the Lizard and there's no knowing who you may bump into.

A few years ago, Anne and I arrived at Cadgwith's gig event early to help unload Falcon and sort out the kit. We also had Fern, our Dachshund, with us, and after doing our bit with the boat, I strolled across the beach with Fern, pausing occasionally while she sniffed enthusiastically around the hulls of the crabbers. Then there she was, Jenny Agutter herself, sitting on the side of an Orkney 13. Just as I would have imagined her, a picture of refined elegance, cashmere sweater and designer jeans. Around her feet were three miniature Dachshunds, and within seconds Fern was exploring their bottoms with ardent curiosity. As I looked at JA, I envied Fern this legitimised ritual of intimacy, confining myself, as custom demands, to a more orthodox verbal introduction.

We passed a few minutes discussing the finer points of Dachshund behaviour. Ms Agutter said when she was not off filming, she liked nothing better than to come down to the cove and take in the unique atmosphere of the Cadgwith's gig racing event. When I confirmed that I was rowing, Jenny said she would watch out for me and bring a towel down to the beach to dry off my sweaty body… no, you're right, she didn't. I am lapsing into fantasy, but the bit about the Dachshunds was true.

If you rowed straight out from Cadgwith and didn't stop you would eventually reach America (you would be bloody tired, though, and remember the Americans do not sell Doombar!). There is no body of land to break the Atlantic swell and the sea comes crashing in onto the rugged Lizard cliffs.

As we started to row out, Brian opined that he didn't like rowing in seas like this. Terry heard him and politely replied, "I am afraid, Brian, it's the only one we have available today", before adding, "so stop ******* whingeing and get on with it you great wussy".

We had a reasonable start. As the flag went up, it was hard enough to keep a straight line in calm water, but in a big swell it becomes a bit of a lottery. So we sneaked a boat length forward, as the others were being told to back up (well, what comes around, goes around). Up to the first buoy we were in the middle of the pack and we turned in tight, in so doing clashing with other crews. The interchanges tended to go something like this:

Our cox... "Fowey, give water; back off". Oars clash and crews have a frank exchange of opinion.

"For **** sake get over... you wankers, give water". Oars start to get lifted like spears and jabbed towards the opposition. An all-out fight is fortunately averted by the need for a final tight turn from Nikki, our cox, that takes us out again into clear water. Then, as we reach the strongest currents between the buoys, Colin let out a fearful oath, and as he did so I saw an oar slide past the bow of the boat and disappear below the crest of the next wave.

"Ignore it, row on," I shouted enthusiastically.

Terry begged to differ.

"Don't be such an ass. These oars are £200 each. Turn this boat around and let's get after it".

So Nikki turned into the big swell and we set off at right angles to the other boats. By this time the oar had floated quite a long way out. It therefore took some catching as the sea was getting rougher and less predictable. I could feel Peter's anxiety and predictably he started his usual muttering. I caught only snippets along the lines of, "who's ******* idea was this? It's just a bloody oar for God's sake, isn't my life more important than an ******* oar?"

"Shut up Peter, concentrate, and just pull harder". I caught Terry's sage advice.

By this time the waves were breaking over the bow and it was getting decidedly cold and wet. Eventually we did get hold of the oar, and pulled it on board... not easy to do this and keep the boat straight in rough water. By the time we turned around we could see the last boats finishing. It was going to be a wet, cold and lonely row in.

But anyone who knows Cadgwith anticipates the compensation to be had through an evening of socialising, singing and imbibing in the imaginatively named pub, the Cadgwith Cove Inn. The majority of our crew were camping that night. There being thick cloud cover, it was the darkest of nights and as no one had thought to take a torch to the pub, the route back to the campsite was followed with much stumbling, knee twisting, and falling into deep ditches. Still, at least the bruises wouldn't register until the next day.

In the morning, Terry, Nikki and Nigel were up cooking breakfast. An unselfish act, but also a useful way of enticing everyone out of their tents, as all hands would soon be needed to put the boat away. By 10.00am the majority of tents were down, and the happy campers had assembled by Terry's truck.

Except, that is, for Dr John. From his tent there had been no movement, no stirring, no response to the aroma of sizzling bacon. Megan tried to awaken him by shouting through the canvas, but to no avail. This was obviously a man with a really serious hangover. He was no doubt feeling awful, if he was feeling at all. Terry showed typical sympathy for his suffering colleague's plight...

"John, JOHN get out of that tent now, before we pull it down on top of you. The boat needs putting away, remember that thing we were floating in before we got pissed... And we need everyone to help".

Still no response. Well there is no point in making idle threats. Megan and Gemma pulled out the outside pegs before trying to rouse John one more time. Now there was a stirring and a growling, "Go away you lot, bugger off, leave me alone... I need to sleep".

Oh dear, Dr John, not the required response. The rest of the pegs came out and the poles caved in. A few seconds later a livid figure came crashing out from the wreckage, not a pretty sight, frothing at the mouth as he spat out threats and expletives.

(It sounded good entertainment... a bit like matadors poking a bull).

Apparently John never did lend a hand with the boat. No, he drove off in a shower of mud, swearing vengeance and lifelong abstinence from Devoran Pilot Gig Club.

6.30pm Tuesday, training time and John's there right as rain and rearing to go. Sunday morning? What Sunday morning?

Points of Interest

In the 19th Century gigs would often be away from their home port for days and nights on end in search of pilotage. During bad weather it has been reported that the crew members would pull their gig up onto the shore before turning upside down to provide a night's shelter.

This practice has happened in more recent years but only as a desperate measure and invariably following over indulgence on local ale.

Chapter 12
Fowey and a Shredded Right Hand

Points of Interest
Location
Ancient South coast port built on famous trade route to Ireland. Forms eastern end of the Saint's Way.

Gig Club
The River Fowey Gig Club. Initially in the 1980s gigs such as Active were borrowed from Newquay as interest and membership developed. The first gig, Rival, was built by Ralph Bird in June 1989. Two other gigs have followed, Gallant, 1996, and Lantic, 2003. The former was named after a band of villains famous for pillaging French ports: The latter after the local dredger, Lantic Bay.

Rowing Conditions
A race of two parts. Sheltered conditions within the narrow estuary, but the sea livens as the gigs leave the mouth of the river.

Pub Check
Recommended for a pub crawl. My favourite remains the King of Prussia, partly for nostalgic reasons!

Tourist Interest
Stunning location, many buildings of historical interest, smart restaurants and even smarter shops. Ferries run regularly to Polruan, Bodinnick and Mevagissey.

Best Experience

Finishing the race each year as it always seems a very long way up the estuary on the last leg.

Fowey is an ancient port situated on the east side of Cornwall's south coast. It grew from the early settlements that were made at the river mouth. Traditional half-tiled fishermen's cottages line the winding cobbled streets that lead down to a picturesque waterfront. This faces across the river mouth to the small village of Polruan.

I can personally vouch for the fact that Fowey is built on some of the steepest hills in Cornwall. The road down from the car park is at such an acute angle that I recently had to ascend it on all fours. However, my colleagues have since confirmed that this was as a consequence of a serious night of Doombar consumption in the legendary King of Prussia. Colin observed that several elderly ladies walked past us in a vertical position. No, not our women's B crew, even older than that! If you look about Fowey you can see that the very ancient locals are either culled early or go on to acquire calf muscles like footballers.

This is a relaxing tranquil spot, or would be without the constant banging and droning from the up-river dock end side of town. Here they load and unload the china clay, Cornwall's 'white gold'. This powder is a ubiquitous substance that seems to have a role in the manufacture of everything from glass to false teeth. As you drive down the A30 into Cornwall you will notice a white mountain range just outside St Austell. Don't get excited and reach for the crampons and skis, these are old china clay slag heaps. Still one of the redundant old quarries was put to good use by a certain enterprising Mr Tim Smit and became transformed into the glorious biomes of the Eden Project.

Fowey is now getting very trendy and in the centre of town it is easier to find a shop selling a pair of designer Italian shoes than a loaf of bread. It has also increased its tourist season by the creation of the Fowey literary festival founded partly on the back of the town's association with such literary heavyweights as the former resident Daphne Du Maurier and the regular visitor Kenneth Graham of the *Wind In the Willows* fame. (I am writing this only so I can get an invite next year and share my chapter 'The Wind In The Gig Shed, a Sunday morning hazard for gig rowing folk', before returning to the beer tent to avoid having to talk to real intellectuals like that Melvyn Bragg.).

I also hear that Fowey is getting a bit of a reputation for the sophistication of its culinary arts. I can see that because the cheesy chips at the King of Prussia are just perfect after a long, knackering gig course and form a good base for the Doombar onslaught. But if you prefer to pay 50 quid for a few lettuce leaves then I am told that all tastes are catered for.

Another feature of this port is the imposing ruins of St Catherine's castle, a defensive fortification built by Henry VIII. It is rumoured that he brought his wives down here to bond with them in the clear Cornish air. When they fell out after two days of such close confinement, his Majesty carriaged them swiftly back to the Tower of London to settle the argument decisively in his favour. When Henry threatened to give you the chop, the man wasn't mouthing idle metaphors. (It is said that there is still a male school of thought in the St Austell area that sees Henry as a role model for his uncomplicated and decisive approach to the resolution of domestic dispute.). Just to think if he had taken up those offers from the sixteenth century marriage guidance service the course of history could have been altered.

So, I always look forward to returning to Fowey to row although it is a deceptively long and challenging course. The gigs are moored below the small car park at the jetties just east of the car ferry to Bodinnick. The course of the race is from this point up through the main harbour and out past the river mouth into the sea. Two long turns are then negotiated before the gigs begin the long home leg back past the esplanade and the waterfront housing. It takes approximately twenty-five minutes depending on conditions but can feel even longer. This I think is due to the position of the finishing point right up the river at the far northern edge of the town.

Rowing has always been seen in popular imagination as a character building activity along with boxing, being in the army cadets, and running up Dartmoor Tors, but faith in Devoran Pilot Gig Club as a nursery for the development of stoicism and resolve in adversity was temporarily shaken during a recent event at Fowey.

Arriving late for our B crew race (a common occurrence), Dr John was told to pick up the stroke-side '2' oar, as opposed to his usual bow-side '3' oar – the reason being that we had too many bow-side rowers and therefore needed one of the crew to switch.

John, glowering at the captain, jerked the oar off the ground, muttering under his breath. I just picked up "why me" and "not fair" as it drifted by on the westerly breeze. We got in the boat in the appointed order and started rowing around the River Fowey for several minutes, loosening up as the starter boats got organised.

From just behind me I heard an oar banging down between the pins and a verbal diatribe inclusive of "sodding" and "awkward". The next moment we were called up to the line and the flag went up. I was half aware of the cox going through her pre-race routine – "right lads, deep breaths, total focus, oars just above the water, any second now... "

Suddenly, a familiar voice behind me cut through the tension, "That's it, I can't do this and I won't. I am not rowing, not here. Let me out the boat".

Five heads turned towards Dr John, who had pulled his oar in and had adopted a sour expression common to thwarted adolescents.

I struggled to give eloquent expression to the crew's collective view.

"**** John... the ******* race is just about to start, what the **** are you playing at?"

As John stared resolutely ahead, I jumped up and held up my hand to try and stop the flag going down. I shouted at John to go into my place as I clambered down the boat.

As the flag fell, we all clashed oars as I, having never rowed that side, struggled to work out which hand should be doing what, where and when. We slowly progressed down the river in a hail of spray and windmilling wood.

After the first 300 hundred strokes (well I probably completed only 250) we had fallen about forty to fifty yards behind the majority of the other crews. This was not a surprise. But then I was aware of another cox shouting nearby. "Come on, ten more, drive her on, let's break the Falcon".

To my amazement, we were alongside William Peters, the Roseland gig. This race within a race continued right around the course, the coxswains, like desperate jockeys, intent on flogging their charges to within an inch of their lives...

"More weight... keep it together, drop it in Dan, you're hanging up". Fortunately Ruth's instructions were partially lost in the strong headwind. Past the crowds cheering on the quay and desperate, so desperate, for that final hooter. At last, this time it sounded for us and we dropped forward in the boat, oars now limp. Three cheers for the William Peters, a "hooray" hardly audible, like a schoolboy concluding the Lord's Prayer.

"Enjoy that John?" I asked with an ironic grin as we clambered together across the lines of moored boats. "It worked out all right didn't it, Dan?" responded John cheerfully as I inspected my shredded right hand.

As I stood on the pontoon, I recognised George pulling his oar in off the William Peters. George, although now in his fifties, rowed for Truro before moving to the Roseland.

He was a highly committed and competent rower. How could he have just been in a crew beaten by one of the weakest Devoran crews in living memory? I wandered over. "**** George, what were you all doing out there? We beat you for Christ's sake, with me on the wrong side". Before he had time to answer I continued:

"No, I get it... it's one of those betting scams. You all made a pact to deliberately throw it and now you're all going down to William Hills to cash in. Next week it'll be Porsche Carreras all round".

George put a hand on my shoulder:

"I wish, I wish. Actually Dan", he continued. "We had Brian over there rowing stroke. He's just had a hip operation. He nobly tried to push off only one leg but found that the anaesthetic hadn't worn off.

"Then Simon, the lad getting out the boat now, he rowed five. The problem is he's a novice, been in a gig twice and the whole thing remains a total mystery to him.

"Then there's Cedric still slumped over in the boat. That's my wife with him now taking his pulse. The silly bugger's pushing sixty and waiting for a bypass operation. He just won't, or can't, give up. His mantra is, 'If I die on the job, so be it'.

"Now, in contrast, Peter, climbing the ramp over there, is only 13. He's going to be a good lad but at the moment his feet don't reach the stretcher and he hasn't got the strength to push the oar right back".

"Okay George", I interrupted. "I've heard enough. I accept that you were in effect rowing it on your own, but at the end of the day, as far as we're concerned, we beat you – another scalp to Devoran and more than enough reason for an extreme celebration".

I picked up my oar and bounced up the ramp from the pontoons to the car park and moved across to our party. The women were sitting on rucksacks against the wall and the men were unscrewing water bottles and tearing open chocolate bars.

All except that is for Adam. He was standing to one side with his hands on his hips vomiting onto the Tarmac and across the bonnet of a white Mondeo carelessly left in his line of fire. A violent convulsion as his body rocked him forward once more to discharge more unwanted fluid.

"Bloody hell", commented Nigel wearily. "A few social beers with us last night and look at the state of him. When is he ever going to learn?" Then I heard Jerry's voice imbued with more urgency…

"Ad, that guy striding over here, the one with the tattoos and the scarred face, I'm not sure that he appreciated your attempt to respray his car yellow and orange. I think he liked it white, the colour it was". Ad appeared to be paying little attention but was gently swaying, hands clasped to knees. Jerry continued:

"Ad, he looks a bit of a psycho to me. I thought they'd eradicated rabies but he's certainly frothing, Ad… "

"Water, water", groaned Adam. "Just give me some… "

"Sorry Ad", cut in Jerry. "We're giving the last bottle to this gentleman to clean his car. You never know our generous gesture could be enough to save your teeth".

At this point I put my arm around Ad and helped him over to the wall. He slumped down onto a coat, breathing slowly and heavily. I bent to put a jumper under his head and to flick gravel out of his ear.

The majority of the women had been stood around watching. Gig rowing is not a fertile recruiting ground for the Mother Teresa, Mission of Mercy brigade. I'm beginning to think that if I had a full-on coronary in the middle of the car park the only response would be Nikki's voice demanding that somebody, "Pull him out of the way will you, the gig trailers need to come through here in a second".

Within half-an-hour, Ad was up on his feet and

following us down towards the British Legion club in the main square. It was time for the traditional Fowey post racing celebrations… a pint of warm Doombar, served in a plastic glass, in one hand and a steak pasty in the other. (I'd always marvelled at how dogs could wolf down the same food day after day with such obvious enthusiasm. The Cornish pasty is the human equivalent).

In front of us, musicians from the Bodmin Brass Band were unpacking their instruments. Devoran are camping again tonight. Ad needed to pace himself as the night was yet young… "that's it Ad, hair of the dog, there's a good boy", encouraged Nigel. Already I could see the colour returning to his cheeks.

Points of Interest

In the late 19th Century generous prize money was available at rowing regattas and as transporting the boats overland was difficult, if not impossible, the crews would often have an arduous row around the coast on the Friday night to be ready for Saturday's racing. These races were often as long as six miles. The crews might then have to row to their home port.

R H C Gillis's research has confirmed that on account of the very big prize money demanded at some regattas there was not always a category for pilot gigs.

However, when gig racing did occur, it was often fiercely contested. For example, at a regatta at Falmouth in 1866, the Fury, Nelly, Energy and Little Sally raced and finished in that order. Subsequently, a heated dispute took place about the legitimacy of the result and it was therefore ordered that the race should be re-rowed. Only Energy and Little Sally would race again, and the former won.

Chapter 13
Fame at Last

One row at Fowey was more bizarre than most. The reason? Just as we were about to get into the gig a bloke with a massive camera on his shoulder pitched up behind me and followed us on board – different to say the least. Once the crew had got over the shock, their immediate collective response was less than enthusiastic. If he expected six Devoranians to hold out their hands and say, "welcome aboard mate, where can we take you?" then the response of certain crew was a little disappointing.

In fact, Brian's mood turned so incendiary he let out a tirade of expletives. The problem was we were not primed for the fact that we were about to have our Andy Warhol fifteen minutes of fame. It turns out that ten minutes or so earlier Terry had been asked, if we, that is Devoran B crew, would be willing to provide a boat and crew as a platform from which said cameraman could film a local feature on gig rowing for use in Cornish schools. Now to most people, Terry's response might have been quite rational along the lines of, "well I'll consult the crew and get back to you", but faced with Claire, a woman possessed of not inconsiderable female attributes and a smile to melt an Arctic glacier, Terry's resistance dissolved with the rapidity of an ice cream in a microwave. Claire, who organised this initiative, is an experienced fellow rower, who maybe thought we were a hospitable lot, or more likely concluded that as we were hot favourites to lose the race anyway we might as well be rowing around with an additional 14 stone body and his assorted, bulky equipment.

Well, the 'hospitable' B crew were only just prevented from walking out of the boat by a late intervention from Terry and Colin (being democrats, they not unreasonably felt that they would like to have been consulted about this additional non-paying passenger). Personally, I thought it was different having a soundboom hitting my head (for I was in the bow) and, hey, the whole thing was rather cool. I nearly ran back to borrow some Oakleys from Jerry, who was waiting with the A crew. As we approached the start-line my mind kept fantasising that we were being filmed because of our rowing expertise. Surely that's what all those watching tourists would be thinking… or maybe this was to be part of a sequence in a Bond movie. A shark-shaped submarine was going to surface among us? I also recalled that the all-action guy who married that Demi Moore started his film career by wearing a vest… quite similar to mine, in fact.

As we got to the start-line I tried to reassure our vilified visitor that the comments drifting down on the wind were not personal. Brian and co were just getting in their raw meat racing mode. Normally they'd have been calling me a "******* burden", it was quite routine language. Well, as I had feared, the race itself proved rather a non-event. The chances are we would barely have been competitive anyway, but with the additional weight there was no chance.

I hear that the start sequence worked out OK with lots of sound and fury, splashing, shouting and so on. But then we sadly fell behind and the noise and the colour quickly diminished. I am ashamed to say that certain crew members let their heads drop and hardly gave it their all. We turned the first mark in near silence, forty yards behind our nearest competitors and the gap continued to widen. From this point I remember thinking that I only hoped he had a strong zoom lens if he needed to get clear pictures of a competitive gig race.

As he disembarked, I did the English thing and thanked him for his time while Brian resumed his swearing and cursing mode from the middle of the boat. Roughly translated, I think he was suggesting that this race had not fully maximised the efficient use of his time (but think four letter words and a pithier sentence structure). A second later his oar flew past me and crashed to the ground. Well, how churlish. We aren't often gifted a cast-iron excuse to be last and the additional bonus of being an inspiration to the next generation! Now school children throughout Cornwall might be fortunate enough to catch glimpses of my sweaty, frayed rowing vest (yes, at least I kept it on). Presumably the sound effects will be expedited and dubbed over, Brian's words being replaced with more polite comments along the lines of, "nice day for it chaps, so let's go out and give it a whirl and see if we can put one over on these Falmouth boys".

Still, it certainly provided a rich subject for ongoing banter. Now, every time Brian gets in the gig in front of me I create another imaginary passenger who is about to join us. "Oh, God, Brian, I didn't know that Terry had agreed to the local coastguard having a lift to the first buoy"; or "the Custom and Excise man's climbing aboard for a tour of the harbour". For our Kippers and Guinness Christmas row I have got plans to get a mate to dress as Santa Claus and follow us, sack over his shoulder, into Falcon loudly repeating "Ho Ho Ho" into Brian's ear.

Chapter 14

Mevagissey and the Missing Crew

Points of Interest
Location
During the past century, Mevagissey was the biggest and most important fishing village within St Austell Bay which lies on the south Cornish coast. Only relatively recently were the fish smoking sheds by the harbour replaced with tourist shops and fast food outlets.

Gig Club
Mevagissey rowing club was founded in 1988. Their first boat, Endeavour, was built by local boat builders, Tom Dudley and Peter Foard. She was launched in April 1988. In 1990, a second gig, Sowenna, was built by Peter Moor.

In 1996, due to the difficulty of boat launching and storage, the gig club moved its permanent base to Pentewan Sands. In recent years, the pretty cove of Portmellon has often been used for training and annual regattas.

Rowing Conditions
Launching can be difficult given an easterly wind and the event has to be held when the water is not too high. During high tides the water can sometimes cover the road. Sea conditions outside this small cove can quickly deteriorate.

Pub Check

Make the most of the Rising Sun in Portmellon during the summer months for as I once found to my cost it is closed in the winter. In Mevagissey, I would recommend the Ship Inn or the Mermaid.

Tourist Interest

Mevagissey is considered one of the most picturesque fishing harbours in Cornwall. Attractions include an aquarium, museum, fishing trips, a ferry to Fowey, restaurants and craft shops.

Best Experience

Watching the Devoran junior crew win their first regatta.

The guide books will tell you that this is one of the most well known and idyllic fishing villages on the Cornish south coast. A cluster of narrow streets lead down to a natural harbour once famous for the volume of pilchards caught by the local boats. Before UK distribution, the pilchards were salted and then pressed into barrels by fishwives. As well as a source of food, pilchards provided oil which was used in lamps for light and warmth. Hence the local rhyme, "Food, heat and light, all in one night".

I visited Mevagissey regularly as a child and recall the fishing sheds along the front and the large volume of brightly coloured fishing boats that clustered in the protected inner and outer harbour. At night, the boats would go out with lights on to attract the sprats. The mackerel would follow the smaller fish right into shore and be visible to the naked eye 'boiling' yards from the beach. It was a daily entertainment to see the fishing boats unload their catch, the cod, pollock and whiting being much sought after.

How things have changed. The only live fish you are likely to see now are in the antiquated aquarium. The cod in the fish and chip shop has probably come down by van from Grimsby.

The once quaint streets are now packed with trinket shops and over priced clothes boutiques. Tourists in Union Jack T-shirts and ill-fitting shorts mill about, throwing chips towards the increasingly corpulent herring gulls. (If the tourist board do want to employ me, I enclose my email address).

As for the protection of the environment, the conservation of our architectural heritage (pass the Kleenex, I'm going to cry). New houses have been built recently on the fields behind the harbour. These are big houses, out of character with their surroundings and painted strident colours just in case the shortsighted might miss them.

This new estate has dramatically altered the visual aesthetic of the town. The local planning department take a bow. I just hope these people don't get jobs managing world heritage sites abroad. I can close my eyes and envisage several scenarios:

near Cairo... oh yes, I reckon that I could just squeeze in a few pebble-dash bungalows between those two pyramids.

mid-Australia... yep, there should be room for a mini-industrial estate in front of that pile of red stone. And who's got the quarrying rights?

Manchu Pichu, Peru... now this lacks facilities and would definitely be improved by a McDonald's (if the Incas hadn't been so obsessed with human sacrifice they'd have come up with the idea themselves).

To re-emerge from rant to rowing event.

A few years previously, the course had been set to start some 200 yards out from the harbour. It went straight out to sea, around two buoys some 600 yards apart and then progressed to a third turn just around the headland in front of the hamlet of Portmellon. Prior to the start of the men's A crew race, our lot had rowed around to Portmellon to avail themselves of the excellent facilities at the pub there behind the tiny harbour wall. The A race was being called up and still there was no sign of them. A 'phone conversation confirmed that they had misjudged the time and couldn't now make it back, prompting sympathetic comments from the women's crew along the line of, "typical, bloody pissheads, more interested in their beer then the rowing club".

Anyway the men's A race started, accompanied by the normal shouting and our thrashing. We then turned away to find our own oars for the next race – the men's B. Ten minutes later and we heard a shout from the harbour wall. It was reported that the Devoran men were leading the pack home. We rushed to the nearest vantage point and sure enough Terry, Nigel and the other lads were steering in just ahead of Fowey. The hooter sounded, the Devoran oars went up, but instead of three cheers, rude and threatening gestures were being directed towards our boys. The embarrassing truth had already dawned on us. The buggers must have just joined in for the last leg like public school boys cheating in the cross-country run. Oh my God, the humiliation. I instinctively found my hand covering my Devoran badge. Terry emerged, leading the crew up the iron ladder by the harbour wall. The smell of alcohol was overwhelming. He looked flushed and flustered.

"What's wrong with these people. Have they no sense of humour. The whole bloody lot of them need to lighten up a bit". He then turned to the rest of the crew, "Right lads what'll it be?"

Well, I thought it was funny, but the gig rowing hierarchy took a dim view and threatened us with suspension and bans and floggings and all sorts of nasty things. However, our committee grovelled long and hard and we were let off with a warning and put on probation with regard to our future conduct.

We informed Terry and he replied with an exaggerated belch.

The party had already started in the Ship Inn so why waste time on recriminations?

Points of Interest
The Racing Rules of the Cornish Pilot Gig Association

Turning Marks

1. *On approaching a mark, when the bow of an inside gig gets ahead of the coxswain's position of another gig, (an overlap), the inside gig has right of way. The outside gig must give the inside boat enough water to turn the mark without being impeded. Umpires must decide who has right of way six lengths from the mark and inform each crew via a loud-hailer.*

2. *A gig approaching another gig which is already turning a mark, must pass on the outside of that gig or wait until that running gig is clear.*

In Open Water

1. *An overtaking gig must keep clear of a gig being overtaken.*

2. *A leading gig must maintain a straight course*

and not zig-zag with the intention of impeding a following gig.

3. Coxswains should endeavour to avoid collision at all times. They should try to anticipate collision situations and take avoiding action in good time. Coxswains should instruct their crews to stop rowing or stop the gig if necessary to avoid impact.

Start

The start for all heats will follow the same routine. The start flag will be raised to indicate that the gigs are under starter's orders. When the starter is satisfied that a fair line has been achieved, the flag will drop. Any crew found in front of the line despite requests to get back, will be disqualified.

Chapter 15
A Champion at Last

Gorran Haven means many things to many people – and probably nothing to the majority of you! A small fishing village three miles to the west of its more famous neighbour, Mevagissey, it boasts a fine granite harbour wall, two small, sandy beaches, a central huddle of traditional Cornish cottages and the inevitable signs of more recent development, pebble-dash bungalows encroaching up the hillsides.

This is the holiday destination of my childhood, the culmination of a six hour journey from Bristol, during which I regularly threw up in my mother's lap. Recollections include, huge, basking sharks hanging from the harbour wall (gruesome trophies for the tourists); fishing off the rocks towards Dodman Point; moonlight walks along the cliff path; and long sessions in the Llawnroc hotel... and you think you had an exciting childhood?

So to return each year for a rowing event is a real pleasure and in between races I can be seen standing on the quay or wandering the coast path rapt with nostalgia.

The members of Gorran Pilot Gig club remind me of Devoran. They are sociable, loud and hospitable, essentially undeterred from having a good time in the bar by their mediocrity on the water.

So the rowing event is great but for once this is not the highlight. It's overshadowed in the evening as the

112

Llawnroc Hotel hosts one of the high points of the Cornish 'events calendar', the County Hay Bale Tossing Competition (yes, all accommodation is booked years in advance). As soon as the boats have been put away, hundreds of rowers congregate in the large gardens of the pub to resurrect this rural skill, and lock metaphorical antlers in a sweaty, testosterone fuelled contest with no quarter asked or given. All this to the floodlit backdrop of a sizzling pig roast, providing drop dead scrummy pork and apple sauce rolls. The garden also boasts two much-needed additional bars.

The challenge is created by the provision of two high vertical poles supporting a movable horizontal bar. Over this a formidably large and compact hay bale must be thrown by pitch fork. This is a contest for both sexes, the men competing first. Terry has a good record, a background of farming and mining having given him enormous strength. Our captain limbers up by demolishing a row of pints generously donated by his devoted Devoran following. Nikki then starts massaging his neck.

Aspiring competitors pay their entry fee and sign their names in the tent. The bar is placed at around six foot, the entry height. The tannoy calls up the first competitor.

Some milk the applause, theatrically flexing their muscles and waving at their partisan support. Others react more nervously, head down and serious, stabbing the bale as soon as they can, throwing it and retreating quickly to their seats. With fifty-odd competitors there this is always going to be a long night. A Cadgwith man throws himself off his feet; the bale lands back on the head of a man from Polgooth; for young Simon from our crew the bale won't leave the fork and returns embarrassingly to his feet; George from Praze releases the fork and the bale simultaneously and to a great cheer everything flies over the bar.

Terry has been going well but then slips as he heaves the fork and bale up towards the ten foot bar. This alters the trajectory and the bar crashes down. Unluckily, this is a one chance saloon and the moment has gone. Disappointment, commiseration from the Devoran ranks.

But then, up steps young Adam, still a contender in what looks like being the final round. A great effort just falls short. Nine others also fail at around fifteen feet and so it's left to the local man from Mevagissey to make a name for himself. Back to the bar, eyes narrow, fork digs in, a drive up from the legs and over it sails... The men's winner takes a bow as the Mevva boys go wild.

Now it's the women's turn. A trickle approach the tent. But will any Devoran women enter? Suddenly, and quite unexpectedly, Anne makes her move. Without a word to anyone else, she enters the tent and returns to her seat. I look on in wide-eyed astonishment. "I used to do this for a living", the tone is calm, phlegmatic. "I didn't get these shoulders from crochet, did I?"

The first woman is called. She strides out, sticks her fork in the bale and screws up her face. Nothing moves, least of all the hay. Another lunge accompanied by a noise like a constipated goat. Still no joy. Amid a few supportive calls inclusive of "hard luck Sue, too much shagging last night?" and "drink another cider", the first competitor slinks back to her table with an exaggerated shoulder shrug.

Two more aim at this height – a girl from Caradon swinging herself round in a full circle and a Falmouth crew member clattering the bar. The tannoy crackles back into life "Anne from Devoran". Anne walks confidently forward, one deep breath, a strong grip on the fork, an upward push, a flick and over the hay bale soars. Feet stamping and cheering from the Devoran contingent.

The competition hots up. A huge girl in a lime green singlet sets the pace; grunting with the effort and roaring at her every success.

Anne stays in there, almost unnoticed. Quiet and efficient, focused and determined. Just five competitors left. The bar's cranked up and the first three girls can't clear it. Now there's just the green giant and Anne to go. Tessa jogs up and milks the applause.

A towering figure, she spears the bale with the casual ease of a cocktail-stick waving child spearing a sausage. Tessa adopts a crouching position, then lunges up. The bale sticks on the end of the fork, it teeters, catches the lip and down the bar comes with a metallic clank. Tessa curses and sighs, scuffing the ground as she moves away.

Anne approaches. Devoran have now mounted the tables and are banging their feet. The chanting starts.

"Give us an 'A'; give us an 'N'; give us another 'N'"… a pause and Anne turns her head and shouts "and another 'E'". The volume increases. "GIVE US ANOTHER 'E', what have we got? ANNE! Go Anne! Go Anne! Go Anne!"

A deep breath, a firm grip on the handle, a quick look up at the bar and a strong drive from the legs. The arms extend, the wrists jerk forward. Time seems suspended as the bale hovers in the air, then it turns forward, flicks the bar and crashes down the far side. The bar wobbles, but stays put. The Devoran contingent erupts. "CHAMPION, CHAMPION, CHAMPION! Give us an A, give us an N… "

As Anne returns, wreathed in smiles, we all start bowing and walking backwards before her. The drinks are lined up on the table. Terry articulates our feelings, "you beauty! Queen of the tossers, Devoran's very own champion!"

As the clammer subsides, I am tapped on the arm, and recognise a London accent. The smart clothing gives the origin away.

"Hi, we're just down from Richmond on holiday for the week. Is this how you entertain yourselves every weekend in Cornwall?"

"Oh yes," I reply, "next week it's the Mevagissey mackerel juggling tournament, followed in a fortnight by the Devoran pasty throwing contest... a very prestigious event. Surely they compete in London?"

An uncertain look in response, followed by a rapid return to the gin and tonic.

I hear Anne phoning our daughter Claire to share the good news. Claire called it "Mum's 'destiny'. A culmination of a life's work… the glory of a youth spent truanting on farms".

The prize? Strangely, a bottle of vodka, but who's complaining? We're all camping and Devoran's finest always need a nightcap to rock them off.

A few years ago, the Llawnroc Hotel was also the venue for one of Devoran PGC's more infamous episodes. As usual, the Cornish sports were continuing long into the evening and the pub garden was packed with thirsty rowers and bewildered tourists. At around

11.00pm several of us remarked on the prolonged absence of Terry (believe me, if he is not there you do notice), how he would *never* take that long to get a drink... so where was he?

Jerry claimed that he had seen him walk off in the direction of the car park... probably to avoid the queue in the pub and have a pee in the hedge. So Jerry set out to take a look. Ten minutes passed and Jerry had not returned. Now for these two, a prolonged absence from the bar area as last orders approached was not normal behaviour. What was going on?

Doctor John was sent to find out. He marched off into the darkness and we waited expectantly for news. The next thing we heard was a distant call for help, so we rushed off across the grass in the direction of the cry. But as we approached, Dr John shouted an abrupt warning, "mind the ditch, mind the ditch. I've got two injured bodies down here".

Sure enough, just the other side of a low dry-stone wall we came across a deep hollow in which we could just make out the hunched, groaning bodies of Terry and Jerry. Dr John was kneeling down administering to them. The likely prognosis... a broken rib cage in Terry's case; a suspected broken ankle for Jerry... the call went out to send for a bottle of whisky. For these two it was to be a long and painful night. So what happened?

Terry, as suspected, had gone over towards the hedge to relieve himself. He had come across the low wall, jumped over it and disappeared straight down into a ditch lined with jagged lumps of granite. Jerry... well, he heard Terry calling and did exactly the same. Straight over the wall and over on his ankle. Dr John explained that he had nearly ended up in the same state, but just caught Jerry's weak, warning cry before he, too, vaulted the wall.

This resulted in thirty minutes of mayhem, two first team rowers rolling around in agony and the worst part about it, several of us missed last orders trying to find them. But all things considered it might have been even worse. But for Dr John's caution, each individual club member present that night might have staggered off across the pub garden, stepped over the wall and crashed down into the rocky darkness.

It reminded me of those Neanderthal mammoth traps I read about (like Piglet's heffalump trap) except that this one was successfully deployed for pissed Devoran gig rowers.

Chapter 16

The Emptiest Campsite in Cornwall

Arranging a gig rowing event is like an organising a complex military operation and recent publicity has reminded us how disorganised a battleground can be – aren't the majority of troops killed inadvertently shot by their own allies? Each year in July the nightmare scenario recurs. Devoran PGC has to get sorted to cater for the arrival of twenty-odd gig clubs with their throngs of hungry and thirsty supporters in tow. The complications start immediately.

Our rowing location, Mylor harbour, just east of Falmouth, is shared by the majority of the county's yachtsmen (or is the current terminology yachtspeople?).

The majority of the space on land is taken up with trailers and boat supports and the majority of the space on the water by the yachts themselves. Saturdays in summer are also their regular race day so negotiations have to take place to try and secure a space on the water for our rowing course and a clear slipway to launch all the gigs. Immediate potential for chaos and, yes, it has happened that the gig rowers and yachtsmen have arrived on the Saturday both expecting to race across the same stretch of water.

So the planning for all this necessitates many meetings in the office/Old Quay Inn. An event checklist goes on forever. Who's going to: bring the barbeque; collect the marker buoys; lay the course; arrange a start boat and follow boats; prepare the food and serve it; park the cars; unload the boats; remove the trailers and so on? So, over a bevy or two we make a few plans on Monday, a few more on Tuesday and by Friday night it's under control. The problem is, has everyone been assigned a task to make maximum use of their area of expertise? Admittedly difficult in my case.

Last year I was posted to the car park with a two-way radio and a cash float. I don't know why everyone assumed I knew how the thing worked, but I did eventually pick up that if you randomly pressed buttons communication would cease. Spatial awareness not being a prime strength, the field soon filled up in less than orderly manner. My assistant Mike remarked that the parking alignment reminded him of the positioning of dodgem cars immediately after the electricity is shut off. (As a result several family cars and assorted gig trailers were blocked in until late into the evening).

I also got to observe at first hand the British reluctance to part with their hard-earned money as I politely explained to our guests we charge £2.00 to park, not to take pleasure in gratuitously ripping them off, but in order to be able to donate £1.00 to the RNLI and to still secure a humble profit for our own club. I was shocked to receive muttered comments of the, "£2.00, a bit bloody steep", or "remind us to charge you at our place next time", variety. As Nikki pointed out, it's cheaper than the metered parking at the harbour (without adding that this option would, however, have saved them a half-mile round trip with pushchair, pram, change of clothes etc.).

My next job was helping my colleagues who were unloading the gigs from their trailers and then rowing them around to the beach in front of the sailing club. Quite an eye-opener seeing the pristine condition of other people's boats and their immaculate, unchipped oars. I joined in dark mutterings of, "Oh just let them try our kit and see how they'd get on. Wouldn't be so easy then, would it... Oh no". But as Anne points out this is rather adopting the wrong perspective, as you can't really blame other clubs for preserving their racing boats in decent condition. No one makes us toss our oars down after a row or scrape the boat across the ground as an alternative to using those custom-made rollers. But as Nikki argues in our defence, the bigger clubs do have three gigs available. This means that there are two to train in during the week, leaving one in the shed just for use on Saturday!

Rowing the gigs around didn't prove quite so easy. With the tide up, it's a very narrow entrance and exit from the launch site out past the moored boats and walkways towards the far beach. When there are only two of you in the boat grabbing any old oar and facing different ways your orientation can get as scrambled as a gig rower's head at a beer festival. I started by rowing one of the varnished boats straight into the wall in front of a horrified audience. The next pride and joy was grounded on the shallow water just ten yards out, where she started being blown across onto her side. As spectators gathered and tempers frayed, I was relieved by Terry of my duties and sent out of harms way to lay out the sandwiches. Fine, anything to help break down the sexual stereotyping.

I don't know if this will surprise you, but Devoran PGC's rowing course is one of the shortest on the circuit of events. A competent crew should be able to row around the three buoys and get back to the beach in about nine minutes. I think the plan is to catch our opponents unaware. For example, the Caradon and Falmouth crews could still be at the warming-up stage when we are going flat out for home. So a simple plan guaranteed to bring success? Er, well it didn't quite work like that! But to be fair, we do better, marginally better, in our own water; the men's and women's A crews coming in the middle of the pack and the B crews doing OK in the middle of the heat in their respective races.

Generally it is to our advantage that the conditions tend to be flat, as the course is laid across the sheltered waters of the Carrick Roads at the mouth of the Fal Estuary. However, a year or so ago, with a strong breeze inducing a choppier sea, we found we had an additional factor in our favour.

The orange marker buoys we had put down to mark the triangular course were held in their place with weights rather than anchors. The result was that just prior to the race, as the wind speed increased, they started moving around and heading towards Falmouth. Trust Devoran to be different and create the first mobile course! As the leading gigs approached the first buoy and the bow rower tossed over the oar to negotiate the first sharp turn, so the marker moved away again. Priceless! Now, as we were aware this was happening we were able to row on well past the buoy before beginning to turn our gig, and as most of the others were infringing the rules by going inside it we could then disqualify them.

We *did* win the Veteran's race. OK, before you ask, Caradon men's veterans didn't enter and we had our men's crew out competing against a majority of mixed crews, but never the less, the fact is we won one of our own cups. Our first chance to finish a race by putting up our oars vertically to signal victory. I was proud to burst... If only my Mother could have been there... and where were the press? The sweet smell of victory in my nostrils... or was that Terry's recycled pasty?

Then it's back to taking a turn on the barbeque, picking up the beer cans and trying to follow the fall-out from the parking chaos.

As is the custom within the gig rowing community we had arranged camping facilities just up the hill from the beach. Being civilised beings, (despite these pages of proof to the contrary) we had even installed four portaloos. The partying was going to be spectacular and the field transformed into a scene from the Glastonbury festival – tents and revellers stretching into the distance.

The reality? Terry, Nikki, Colin and Maria were the only ones to opt for the night under canvas. After a few beers at the sailing club our guests drove off, leaving our few brave traditionalists to the least crowded campsite in Cornwall. Now I don't know exactly what happened, as Anne and I drove back to the 'office' before retiring to our own bed. There were, however, unsubstantiated rumours of gratuitous nudity, skinny dipping and a dawn barbeque. One thing is certain, however, come the morning and there was no need for anyone to queue for the loo.

Chapter 17
Colin, Albert and Edgar

Colin, the chairman of Devoran PGC, is a big-hearted rower and in many other ways an irreplaceable member of the club. This is a man who took up rowing at 41, rowed for the Veterans and then as the years went by worked his way through to the A crew. He's now reversing the process...

But Col is not just valued for his committed contribution on the water or his wise counsel as chairman, he also has a niche as a club entertainer, who specialises in the recitation of historic speeches and comic verse. You never quite know with Colin when he is being serious. He has a very eclectic repertoire and can move from a hilarious rendition of Marriott Edgar's *The Battle of Hastings* to a serious, even solemn, delivery of Abraham Lincoln's great speech of unification, the Gettysburg Address.

Colin is obviously touched by Lincoln's profound words and imbues them with great meaning and authority. To quote the first few lines:

"Fellow Countryman – four score and seven years ago our Fathers brought forth on this continent, a new Nation conceived in Liberty and dedicated to the proposition that all men are created equal... "

To think that politicians once wrote speeches like that with no Alastair Campbells to help them.

But never take a serious Colin for granted, I once asked him to come over and meet some friends of mine and then put him on the spot to deliver 'his' great speech.

"Oh," said Col, "you want the Gettysburg address?" Then, putting his arms to his side and puffing out his chest, he announced,

"5 Acacia Avenue,

Gettysburg,

Pennsylvania,"

before walking off to the bar.

But the poem that stands out as the club favourite is *The Lion and Albert* by the incomparable Marriott Edgar. This is the story of a boy called Albert who visits Blackpool zoo with his parents, annoys a lion and pays the ultimate penalty!

Colin adopts an authentic Lancashire accent and his body language and voice cadence imbue every line with maximum humour. I'll quote the first and last verses and if it interests you I should look it up.

There's a famous seaside place called Blackpool,
That's noted for fresh-air and fun,
And Mr and Mrs Ramsbottom
Went there with young Albert, their son.

...

At that Mother got proper blazing
"And thank you, sir, kindly," said she
"What waste all our lives raising children
To feed ruddy lions? Not me!"

Halfway through the poem, Colin stops and looks up to the ceiling. He rubs his hands across his chin and then announces, "Now let me see, er, um, how does it go?" The audience will him to recall the next line, not to leave us in such suspense. But in reality there is never a chance of Colin's memory failing. Much to the relief of all, he's soon continuing with the same fluency and mannerisms as before. And the voice slows for the final few verses, exacting maximum pathos.

So, there probably aren't many pubs in the country where Saturday night customers are entertained by the Gettysburg address or pre-war Lancastrian poetry. (Well, we don't know or care what you do in the rest of the country. You go to your theatres, cinemas, drive-ins or whatever and we'll just stand in our local pub and get our entertainment for free).

Well, this prompted the thought that we should have a club poetry writing competition in honour of Mr Edgar.

Here is an initial first effort.

Adopt Lancashire accent... or, ideally, enlist Colin:

> *There is a grand gig club in Devoran,*
> *To be found on the south Cornish Coast,*
> *The members they do like their rowing,*
> *But Doombar is what they like most,*
> *In May they all 'ead for the Scillies,*
> *A grand piss-up is there to be had,*
> *The beer it do flow like the Tiber,*
> *To stay sober you'd have to be sad,*
> *Now Terry, he got there on Friday,*
> *Fourteen pints he did put down the 'atch,*
> *The Doombar was sliding down lovely,*
> *A grand total that no team-mate could match,*
> *The racing do cause a distraction,*
> *From the ale that's there to be drunk,*
> *But the cox needs a clear 'ead for coxing,*
> *Or your gig is right liable to be sunk.*

Rowing with my Wife

The sea it can blow up real frisky,
And drive boats up onto the shore,
So it's best to row back some quickly,
To get a round in... and then some more.
The final it 'appens on Sunday,
The gigs all lined up by Nut Rock,
Devoran B are let off in the first 'eat,
First back to the bar, so don't mock.
The Bishop it fills up with people,
With only one thing on their mind,
The barmen keep running like ferrets,
And no sober Devoranian you'll find.
The party it 'appens past midnight,
We all stagger on down to the beach,
The fire burns bright in the moonlight,
As the tinnies are brought within reach.
The morning it comes far too quickly,
Cos' few rowers are sleeping alone,
Another World Championship over,
Pack up gig, board ship, and off 'ome.

Chapter 18
The Great Pushathalon

Terry has assured me that on at least two occasions this season, the Devoran gig, Falcon, has swept past both Caradon and Falmouth gigs. I couldn't recall or imagine this occurring so I decided to seek further clarification. "The Falcon went past the Caradon gig, Miller's Daughter, so quickly it was just a blur", boasted Terry. The answer? Terry was towing our gig down the dual carriageway at breakneck speed (69.99mph) as Miller's Daughter was progressing more sedately in the slow lane.

So we may not be the fastest on the water, but off it, bring it on! (Now, that gives me a good idea for a new trophy).

A natural continuation of this theme moves us to a charity event for CLIC, organised by Nikki, Terry's wife and the ladies' captain. This event, held in Truro on a Saturday in June, is a Pushathalon. Teams from all walks of life enter a pushable vehicle and dress up in response to a specific theme. We did South Sea Islands costumes last year, loud shirts and shorts for the men, and grass skirts and colourful bikini tops for the girls. (It sounded reasonable to me). Our vehicle? The gig on its trailer. Our purpose? To collect as much money as we possibly could as we pushed Falcon around Truro. Being Devoran, though, we decided to set ourselves an additional challenge... to visit every pub on route. After all, pushing a gig a few miles in the sun is hard work, and a man (and a woman) require appropriate refreshment. Our trailer was also the loudest with *Hawaii Five O* blaring out from the speakers, as the girls swayed their grass skirts in time with the rhythm.

Our collector in chief was Jerry, Jezza to his mates, think Cocker Spaniel in need of Barbara Woodhouse. Jezza volunteered to collect the money and ran around manically, bucket in hand, stopping every shopper and tourist to demand a donation. Now, when Jezza explained that he was collecting for a cancer charity the vast majority of people gave generously (Jezza is a charismatic and good looking guy, not beyond using his personal charms to extort cash). Jezza was even collecting from upstairs windows. Eyes and arms heavenwards, he was imploring the young inhabitants to part with their money in such a just cause... It truly was raining pennies from heaven and a tin hat would have come in handy.

As well as stopping pedestrians, he was jumping in front of cars. A commendably committed approach I thought as, with the smell of burning rubber still in the air, another vehicle screeched to a halt yards from his feet. Still, the bucket was filling up and all was going well until he stepped into the path of a gleaming Range Rover. We heard shouting as the driver wound down his window and expressed a decidedly negative opinion about this impromptu interruption to his journey. But Jerry, being Jerry, instead of jumping aside carried on shaking the bucket undeterred.

"Cancer research, give me some money mate, and I'll let you go by".

We saw the car door open and this big guy get out. He shouted something that would be unsuitable before the watershed (and after it come to that) and moved purposely towards Jerry.

"Get out of my sodding way, you little ****".

This man was no pacifist and Jerry's shining white teeth were in grave danger of being depleted in number. Terry and Carl, who had been watching this scene unfold, moved quickly into the road. Terry put himself between Jerry and his protagonist to play the peacemaker.

"Just try it pal, and I'll stick your head up your own ******* exhaust pipe, this is for cancer you miserable git".

Our 'friend's' courage seemed miraculously to dissolve, and within seconds he had jumped back into his Range Rover and started up the engine. As he drove off, our club members used time honoured sign language to show their appreciation of his attitude.

"Wanker," muttered Terry. "Right, Colin, the Old Ale House next, and I've got a fearful thirst, so put your backs into it and push your bollocks off".

Soon after this, the gig got wedged turning a tight corner, but every cloud as they say... As we pushed and pulled the trailer, the manager of the local wine merchants opposite rushed out with samples of malt whisky to help us on our way. So it was straight down the hatch and shoulders to the trailer and not surprisingly this time it moved.

An hour or so later and I was grateful that we had the gig trailer... to lean on. We arrived back at the central square (a piazza now, you know... posh place Truro) as the band was warming up. By now it was full of prams and every sort of improvised vehicle.

The red barrels had arrived back before us; six

figures dressed in red plastic suits pushing around their barrels while making loud aircraft noises.

The hospital trolleys were also coming back with nurses and doctors everywhere. As wielded by the now less than sober doctors, the cold metal of the stethoscopes was being used to probe perfectly healthy areas of their patients' anatomy resulting in prolonged giggling!

Chapter 19
Cawsand and Party-time

One of the main attractions of joining Devoran Pilot Gig Club was their reputation for having a great time après row (okay, another was the fact that we moved there and a third, it was one of the few clubs with whom I could probably get a regular row).

Apparently the key to enjoying the rowing season was to take your tent to every event. None of this, "Oh, I'm sorry I'm driving so I can only stop for a quick shandy", namby pamby talk from our crews. The accommodation was already pegged down and the barbeque at the ready. It's now the case that most clubs do secure a camping field for visiting rowers so that there is no excuse to slink off home.

My first experience of a Devoran night away was at Cawsand/Kingsand. One of the advantages of gig rowing is that you get to explore the south west coast and while Anne and I had walked long sections of it, I had never before been to the adjoining villages of Cawsand and Kingsand. What gems of old world charm they turned out to be. And a setting lying on the Rame Head peninsula, overlooking Plymouth Sound. On hearing about our weekend destination, my brother-in-law Trevor, a naval man, recounted a story of twenty years or more ago. It was just after the film *Jaws* had come out and Trevor, then stationed in Plymouth, decided the holidaymakers on Rame Head needed livening up. One sunny morning with another naval mate he made and attached rubber 'fins' to his and his colleague's shoulders and backside and set off to swim round in front of the beaches. The papers reported that mayhem ensued, children and parents scrambling out of the water and screaming up the beach. Trevor and his mate then discreetly removed their flippers to have a relaxing sunbathe, a beach each to themselves. I told him he was lucky that Robert Shaw didn't pursue him with a harpoon gun!

On the day we were due to camp, it was raining stair rods. The mist had also descended and although the gig rowing continued it was hard to see anything beyond the beach. I don't remember a great deal about the row (for reasons that may become more obvious), just driving forward into a blanket of mist and hoping that someone's cabin cruiser wasn't simultaneously returning to harbour. For some reason the B crew were disqualified, possibly for trying to start forty yards in front of everyone else.

We were all soaked through to the skin and after the rowing retreated to the pub in the main square at Cawsand. A quiet pint and warm-up by the fire. I don't think so. Terry devised this game that made use of a floppy woollen hat that Nikki had produced from somewhere.

The rules were that the person in possession had to plonk it on someone else's head and then kiss them. The receiver then had to find the next victim. Now, being Devoran, such an inclusive lot, the fun wasn't just confined to our club members and Terry soon pulled the hat over the hair of a quiet, elderly lady sat in the corner and plonked a big kiss on her cheek. A hush and all eyes to the right. Was this going to result in a law suit for harassment/assault? But, of course, she loved it with Terry's infectious laugh and arm around her shoulder. "Brilliant, brilliant," he said as she passed it on to someone else and pecked them on the cheek.

At 7.00pm it was agreed to return to the tents for a change of clothes. Unfortunately no other variation on 'getting ready to go out', was available. One portaloo was, however, considerately provided but at a point down by the stream where the mud was knee deep. This was no Eurocamp. The party re-grouped around 8.00pm to take on the challenge of the five pubs conveniently placed within the Cawsand/Kingsand boundary. I remember crowded bars and lots of singing led by Brian, our star baritone. *South Australia* stands out, a sea shanty with a very catchy chorus. (I've heard it hundreds of times but still forget the majority of the words or remember them but in the wrong order!).

Around midnight I wandered off for a few quiet gulps of oxygen and got parted from our group. I presumed as the pubs were shutting they would be heading back to the campsite so, trying to retrace my steps, I made my way back up the hill towards the muddy field. It seemed relatively quiet as I slithered through the mud and found my car. Then I realised, "Oh ****", because it was pissing down earlier on I hadn't bothered to put the tent up. Not to worry, I put down the seats in the Citroen Picasso and prepared to stretch out in my sleeping bag. I shuffled a few things around, moved the Wellington boots away from my head and lay still. I must have dozed off for a bit because I woke up feeling cold and looked at my watch, 1.30am. I could hear the odd murmur outside and a distant radio. Everyone must have turned in and be slumbering in their tents.

Then, as I closed my eyes again, I heard an increasing babble of sound moving closer. Then lights appeared, shouting, raucous laughter. A small army seemed to be on the move but this was more like the peasants' revolt than the seventh light infantry. The next thing a huge searchlight went on in the middle of the field and music started up at deafening volume. The searchlight scanned the field Colditz style before alighting on my car. "Williams!!", I recognised Terry's booming voice, "Get off your arse and up here, it's party time".

By the time I had squelched up there, the huge gas barbeque had been lit and crates of bottles were being unloaded from Terry's van. The order was direct

"Grab yourself a roll, stick a sausage in it and pick up a beer".

By this time, a large group of people were falling about in the mud and slurred stories of the day's events were being retold.

I was then aware of John, Mark and several of the younger rowers sniggering and pointing towards Simon's tent. John proclaimed, "he's got a woman in there. I know he bloody has. He met her in the pub. Rows for Tamar, a bloody cracker she is". He moved towards Simon's tent.

"We know what you're up to Si, go on give her one for me… "

Nigel and I pulled him away. "For Christ's sake grow up will you?", Nige said. "You could have found one for yourself if you'd bothered".

At this point Terry became involved having just caught gist of the conversation. Terry was agitated… one of the club was spurning good hospitality and furthermore being a party pooper.

"Simon," he shouted, "there's beer here".

I tentatively suggested that perhaps he'd found something better to do. Bad mistake. Terry stared at me as if I was mad. *"Better to do*!! **** Dan, there's thirty cans of Skinners here and five pounds of sausages. You can shag any time".

Later that night, or more precisely in the early hours of the morning, Mary, one of our younger female crew, made the nearly fatal mistake of deciding to wade her way through the mud and use the portaloo. Mary locked herself in and then Terry had "a brainwave". After a muttered conversation with several of the remaining male crew, ominously ending in howls of laughter, he turned the spotlight on the portaloo and set off with Nige, Mark and Paul down the field. Within minutes it was up on their shoulders and being carried around the field to the accompaniment of high-pitched female screaming and the sloshing and slopping of liquid. The door swung open to reveal Mary trying to pull her skirt up without plunging seven foot down into the mud. Bad call that one Mary, to powder your nose when the boys were in practical joke mode.

There were no showers on site, so no drunken, amorous males were inclined to pursue Mary towards her tent that night. I hope she slept soundly.

Chapter 20
The Two Pins Trophy

Devoran has never had need of a big trophy cabinet. In the corner of the local pub, the odd golfing plate or darts cup have been on display, but rowing trophies have been as rare as hen's teeth.

So Terry decided we needed to rectify the situation. But how? Were we to be put through 'another' punishing winter training regime, told to give up alcohol and replace pasties with wholemeal pasta? In other words, did we have to try and get fit enough to be able to compete with other crews to try and actually *win* something? Terry allayed these fears. Lateral thinking was what was required. The answer? We would devise our own competition and make our own trophies. Brilliant!

The introduction of a new club, Weymouth, provided a ready made opportunity. They were struggling in their first year of competition to beat anyone else and having just joined the gig rowing fraternity lacked contacts and 'friends'. So we had a few beers with them after one race and then arranged to visit Dorset at the end of the season for a rowing challenge and social weekend. (I have subsequently heard that we didn't ask them if they agreed with this but merely gave them the dates on which we would all be coming). But being generous people we agreed to bring the trophies.

Well, what a weekend it turned out to be. A long night in the pub culminated in wild dancing and striptease on the tables followed by clubbing until the early hours. Relationships were formed and consummated on the beach. Others disintegrated in the bar. The club was subsequently banned from the Seven Winds B&B establishment for disturbing the peace.

But back to the rowing... we won! Probably due to the fact that rowing in a condition my teenage daughter would call "hangin'" is second nature to our lads. We stormed around the course and put the Weymouth 'novices' in their place by at least ten yards! Oars up and savour that sweet moment of triumph.

Terry conducted the post race ceremony. He thanked Weymouth for their hospitality and for letting us win. He then handed out carefully chosen Cornish gifts inclusive of:

'Pasty flavoured edible undies.'

Then to the main presentation. As winning captain, he gave himself a magnificent trophy, consisting of two beautifully carved crossing gig pins on a polished base. This was now to have place of honour in our new 'trophy cabinet' to be admired by all.

The next year Weymouth were due to come to us for a repeat performance. The problem was that during their third season they had started to improve considerably, due to some 'outside coaching' and increased commitment to training. In fact, during the season they had regularly beaten our A crews. Our day of glory looked unlikely to be repeated. Once again, however, Terry generously agreed to provide the trophies for the men's race. On the day this proved closer than expected (probably due to the fact that some of their A crew men had been banned by their wives from travelling). In fact, it almost seemed to me that we eased off towards the end of the race but I banished such thought from my mind. I am sure Weymouth won fair and square.

So to the final ceremony. A round of applause to the winner and then the presentation of a tiny trophy for first place. Then a bigger round of applause for the gallant losers and a huge trophy was wheeled in. The 'Weymouth/Devoran Nearly First Trophy' was proudly unveiled.

"Well," said Terry, amid much laughter, "you buggers didn't actually think that we were gunna let you walk away with all the glory... Just because you were lucky enough to get to the other end slightly quicker than us... "

And the Saturday evening entertainment?

I can't find anyone who remembers exactly what happened.. But the consensus is that it was a bloody good night!

Points of Interest
Gig Club

The first Weymouth gig was built as a memorial to Tristan Douglas Johnson who was killed in a tragic accident on September 22 2000 at the Southampton Boat Show. The idea to create a lasting tribute of this kind, The Tristan Project, was the brainchild of his colleagues at Kingfisher Marine. The gig, Sir Tristan, was launched on the February 6 2001. On March 2 2002 a second gig, Penny, followed, named after Tristan's friend, Simon Penny, who died nine months before him.

This now thriving club operates from the North Castle side of the harbour. Their philosophy is wholly inclusive, to enable people of all abilities to have a go.

The club's attitude is summarised thus "without fun and enjoyment results are only shallow".

Rowing Conditions

Generally calm water within the harbour, and across the shallow, wide bay. However, once the gigs are clear of the protective walls, a brisk easterly can create challenging sea conditions.

Pub Check

Everything happens in the Duke of Cornwall!

Tourist Interest

Massive sandy beach (the shallow water makes it ideal for bathing). Antiquated harbour area; Georgian architecture; museums; sea life centre; butterfly farm; numerous restaurants, pubs and shops.

Best Experience

The trophy presentations; far more imaginative than your normal gig event. The dancing on the tables.

Chapter 21
The Great River Race

A cursory knowledge of history suggests that the only time Cornishmen have headed to London en masse has involved some sort of agricultural rebellion or complaint about taxes and ended in tears and heads on spikes. (So it is probably best to tolerate this year's extra tax on daffodils and the penny on Doombar bitter).

One other more modern invasion was instigated by Cornwall reaching the County Rugby finals. A sea of black and gold then descended upon the capital to support their men from "God's own country" in their quest for Twickenham glory. The pubs rocked to "Oggy, Oggy, Oggy", as Trelawney's Army left no bar stools unused. As the local paper asked, "Will the last person out of Cornwall switch off the lights?"

The annual Thames River Race is now providing another valid excuse for a small-scale migration to the Big Smoke. Friday lunchtime and our cars and the boat trailers head out of Cornwall for a temporary Thames-side campsite, soon to swell to the size of Truro. By dusk on Friday, fields and fields of tents and flags make the final scene resemble a medieval army's last night before battle. The smell of cooking and drinking begins to permeate the air. In short, for the party animals of Devoran Pilot Gig Club this scene has "made in Heaven" written all over it.

Back to the rowing. Saturday's course is twenty-three miles long and stretches from Ham House, north of

Richmond to Greenwich, south of Canary Wharf. More than three hundred traditional rowing craft (drawn from across the globe) will pass through the twenty-six London bridges before reaching their final resting place on the thick mud banks in front of the Poplar Rowing Club. All boats have fixed seats, traditionally built rowing craft so there's no chance of seeing Matthew, James, Steve and Ed screaming past in a Leander 4.

The organisation is acknowledged as brilliant on the water, the boats each receiving a start time that is strictly adhered to. On land it has been more problematic. One functional portaloo for a hundred-plus campers and two cold, dribbling showers. Contracting dysentery has always been more of an immediate danger than drowning.

On the Saturday lunchtime some two hours prior to the start of the race, the crews gather on and around the banks of the Thames in the grounds of Ham House. This provides a colourful and bizarre spectacle. We lined up our two gigs alongside a Napoleonic naval vessel crewed by twelve men in full traditional brass button costume. This was presided over by the authoritative figure of the captain. He stood full square in the stern, hands clasped behind his back, wearing a wide, resplendent triangular black hat.

Next in line was a North Atlantic Whaler, a huge sturdy, thick-planked beast crewed by six flint-hard marines. Alongside this floated a Polynesian Dragon boat like a colourful, aquatic centipede, lines of paddles held by flamboyant looking individuals in South Sea Island dress.

Over to the left were Welsh and Irish coracles, with what looked like black, tar-stained canvas pulled across a wooden skeleton. My attention was drawn to the shore where a group of fully robed, brown-hooded monks were standing around as their boat was unloaded from its rusting trailer. An unusual feature of this scene was the smoke seeping around the edges of their hoods and the spirit bottle rapidly changing hands around the huddled circle. This order of monks was different for sure, more familiar I think with Martinis than Matins.

From behind us, singing and raucous laughter and the great Viking long boat hove into view. This was immediately centre-stage, a magnificent replica with dragon figurehead, propelled by red-bearded ruffians, intent, judging from the bawdy song, on some serious rape and pillage. At first glance it appeared that a naked woman, presumably a hostage, was being passed among the men. I was informed, however, that this was only Priscilla, their team mascot, a well-endowed blow up doll!

Along the towpath, a boisterous, well-toned, all-female crew passed by, buck teethed rodents emblazoned across the front of their T-shirts. As they approached their boat I read the back of one of the singlets, "The Wet Beavers, always up for it whatever the conditions".

Soon it was time to begin to answer that crucial question; what does go through your mind on the brink of such an epic race? What profound thoughts start to dominate as your time draws near? Judging by the urgent but muttered comments of my stroke-side colleague we were on the same wavelength.

"Is there any way out of this boat... I suddenly have a very immediate desire to relieve myself, in fact to flood the nearest urinals". This is not easy in the middle of the

Thames as you are being rapidly steered towards the start-line. The second thought, disturbingly, along the same lines, but possibly more profound. "If my bowels continue to loosen, oh my God I'm going to need a crap halfway down the Thames".

Thousands of people will be supporting, waving, encouraging, watching our every movement. My mind started to race, "it's no good, I'll have to swim to shore… I can't be the first person to appear on regional television at their ablutions". I can imagine the scene. *My* proud mother pointing me out to her friends, "Oh, look there's Daniel – but why's he sitting by himself on that bucket?"

These tortuous thoughts were interrupted by a call over the tannoy for Falcon to come up to the starting line. Listen to the cox, back up together, concentrate, oars forward. Just time for a nervous glance to my right. I register a Viking stubbing out a vast cigar. Flag down, we were off

A rush of adrenaline, breathing in the atmosphere, the wind driving across us, the surge of the tide as the water narrows through the first bridge. Bursting past a four-man craft, the monks in sight, water splashing off the bow oar. London gliding by, on the shore the mansions of Richmond, the elegant fronts at Kew, two more bridges, shirts of black and gold held up like trophies. A clash of oars, too close to the Whaler. The Houses of Parliament, the Eye, come into view. Crowds lining the Embankment, hearing the Cornish Anthem. A voice heard shouting the name of your boat. More Cornish shirts, now six people deep on the Embankment. Senses fully engaged, the pain on hold as we pull on down the majestic Thames, that most famous river, through the heart of the world's greatest city... pure exhilaration.

Bring it on... we're really flying now, so line up the beers!

Fifteen miles down river and Terry announces it's only another seven-and-a-half miles to go. Losing the rhythm, the runners' equivalent of the wall? Terry did you have to point that out, still a distance in excess of twice a normal race? My lips are cracking, my arms and back stiffening, my wrist has stopped feathering the oar. Try and catch a drink with my right hand and notice smeared blood on oar handle. Words of encouragement sought and given from others

"Come on lads, dig in, help each other. Drive forward, lean back, push through the legs, keep it long".

Another gig is approaching and Terry's now seen them out the corner of his eye... he hunches his body towards us, "come on lads, dig in, show some pride. Zennor are catching and we're not going to let it happen. Right, we'll respond... let's have a big ten, suck it in, building for five, one, two... more weight... "

A full on race with Zennor's gig, Senara. Down past Canary Wharf, through the rougher water of Docklands, oars inches apart. Exchange glances... their cox, shouting, swaying forward and back, words of encouragement lost in the wind. Faces mirroring our pain and determination. The name "Falcon" shouted from a fellow boat, dozens of supporters enjoying this race within a race.

And then at last we're doing it... they're slipping away, sliding past our stern. We've broken them. I feel my colleagues relax, but we continue to move away through increasingly brown and choppy water. The river narrows "One more bend", shouts Nigel. I'm half closing my eyes, breathing through gritted teeth, imagining the end. John Mills from the final scene in *Ice Cold in Alex*, that cool lager on the bar. But now the bend's come and gone. "Nigel bloody Pinnock," I shout, "you can row with my oar as well the rest of the way". I feel my head dropping forward at each stroke, my hand is too blistered and sore to hold the oar tight… a back spasm. This time the voice is Terry's…

"That's the finish; it's there… come on let's get it together and do it in style".

"Not a bloody mirage is it Terry?", shouts Colin. "Are there shimmering dancing girls and camels tethered by a palm-ringed watering hole?"

But now I see the crowds, the boathouse, other boats being pulled to shore. We cross the line… I slump forward, arms on Colin's shoulders, Jerry's head's on my back, lips start to crack wider through broad smiles… "Bloody great stuff Col; put it there Jerry".

"****, is that it boys, I was just getting into the rhythm". No response to this feeble quip as water is poured over heads and faces and biscuit packs are ripped open.

Terry's voice again, "right she's drifting with the current. Come on boys, get her into shore for me".

Oars clashing, we heave Falcon across the mud on the east bank and pitch up next to a crew of long-limbed Dutch girls. They are discussing their experience in their native tongue.

Nigel turns to Col and makes a rather lewd comment about the impressive physical characteristics of the woman nearest to him. As Col nods and smiles, the target of their humour breaks off her conversation and swings around to face us. "We speak perfect English, of course we do. So is that what you think of me?"

Crimson faced embarrassment from Nigel. But Helga, as she introduces herself, is in generous spirits and is soon passing over a fine selection of their food supplies. The initial impression is becoming ever more favourable as we share our experiences and marshmallows.

Relieved, exhausted, elated, dehydrated, the next few hours pass in a blur. Up to your knees in Thames mud, staggering to shore, shoes and socks in hand. At last that pint while leaning on the balcony to cheer in our other crew. Comparing hands and aches. The start of the awards ceremony, fastest boat overall (yet again a Dutch monster with seven oars each side), the fastest pilot gig… applause for Helford Rowing Club.

Now time to drain the pint and gather everyone up for the return journey. We head towards the nearest Underground station, following Gemma as she's done this before and is acting as guide. I feel claustrophobic in the Underground, partly relieved by joining in a rendition of *Going up Camborne Hill, coming down*, and other favourite songs from the Devoran repertoire. Multi-cultural passengers look bemused, some apprehensive. Rushing out between stations to the nearest pub, a cavernous, featureless, soulless sort of place. Solitary drinkers sit at the bar and stare straight ahead. Finally Richmond. Crush in four taxis and back to the campsite to light the barbeque. Sausage, steaks, bacon baps. Light headedness recedes and I feel some energy returning. Terry gets the club beer barrel from the back of his truck. Doombar bitter has rarely tasted so good.

Shortly before 10.00pm, Nigel and I lead the rush to the pub. The first and lasting impression is the size of the landlord. Nearly seven foot tall, wider than a London barge and bald as an eagle. This guy reminds me of that villain in the Bond film with the flashing gold teeth. Mental note not to push last orders. We notice with surprise that several other crews have made it before us... perhaps they skipped the solids... we're slipping. Arriving late could damage our reputation.

We squeeze in round a table next to Zennor. Ideal, a solid bunch and we can now bait them about our race. We dismiss their point. OK, they did have two women in their crew but they were experienced rowers and the fact is we still did the business. They rib Sarah from our Fear-Not crew for peeing in a bucket as they rowed past. Apparently this was in front of a packed supporters' boat on one side and the Houses of Parliament on the other. Jed from Zennor gives a graphic description of the impression it made on him.

"On my life maid, it did sound like a loose hosepipe in a tin dustpan. We thought you had a horse on board".

Great banter and then it's my round. I find myself blathering to our Goliath-like publican about the fact that we come from this far flung county of Cornwall. Over the Tamar into a mystical Celtic land etc. Nigel said later that I was talking loudly but slowly to help the 'Eastend local' (aren't all Londoners Eastenders?), get the picture. Eventually he replied, "Yer, I know where it is pal. My Mum lives in Charlestown, near St Austell. I visited last weekend. How many pints of Youngs was it?"

I sat down, climbed into a few more pints of Youngs

and then turned my attention to a table of foreigners on my left (well they certainly weren't speaking English). I leant across and enquired what part of Holland they were from. Unexpected reply: "Are you taking the piss boyyo? We're from Bangor in Wales, you know your Celtic cousins".

Oh ****, yeah, of course, now I recognised that accent. An easy mistake to make?!... and anyway they were far too short to be Dutch.

It's well past midnight and Terry decides that our beer barrel awaits. Nigel and I, the first to the pub, are the stragglers on the way back. As we approach the site we are stopped in our tracks by a primeval scream emanating from the direction of the Devoran camp. We hurry on to find a distraught Terry stamping around the tents.

"Right, which of you bastards out there has got my barrel of beer? Okay, I've warned you. I'm starting here and I'm going to rip up every tent until I find it".

As he approached the first guy line, Nigel, Col and I put a restraining hand on his shoulder and suggested that we start by searching our own camp. Sure enough, the first place we look, there it is covered over in the back of the truck. (The few who stayed behind had obviously put it away).

Beer starts flowing, but our Zennor friends are nowhere to be seen. Terry takes a dim view of Devoran's hospitality being spurned. "Zennor, Mike, Ziggy, you bloody lightweights. There's a party going on here, so get off your backsides, get a glass and help us with this barrel. That's an order".

Eventually, one bedraggled figure emerges from the shadows, glass in hand. A welcoming arm around the shoulder from Terry but where's Ziggy and his mate? Terry turns around in the direction of the Zennor camp.

"Ziggy, you bastard, get out here. Right, I'm going to count to ten and if you're not out of that tent by then I'm going to piss right through it and wash you out the other side".

Ziggy is either comatose, not at home or a brave man. At any event, nothing stirs.

Back to 'the party'. Terry decides that the barrel drinking needs added momentum, so he pulls out a huge plastic funnel from his truck... a cursory wipe of the diesel on his sleeve. This thing appears to be made out of a sliced-off four-pint milk container with attached plastic tubing. Terry strides purposefully towards the barrel, tips it forwards and fills up his new vessel.

"Right, you lot, who's going to be the first man among you to down this lot in one?"

A lot of eye rolling and head turning.

Terry puts his hand on Mark's broad shoulders. "No volunteers? Mark, you can start. Sit down here on the floor and put this tube in your mouth".

Unbelievably, Mark follows this instruction. Half-a-gallon of diesel flavoured Doombar bitter starts pouring down his throat as his Adam's apple works overtime. Job done, give or take half-a-pint of spillage as Terry removes the hose. A few words of encouragement follow. "Good effort Mark, that's my boy"... but we doubt Mark took in a lot of this as he is now writhing on the floor.

"How do you feel?" I enquire compassionately. "Awful, man," groans Mark, before trying to haul himself to his knees only to fall back spread-eagled against the truck's rear wheel. My attention is switched back to Terry.

"Right," he continues. "Come on, who's next?"

"You invented it Terry so I really think it's your turn", I suggest.

"**** you", replies Terry. "Do you think I'm bloody crazy. Look at the state of him".

The only vague memory I have after this was as I was lying in my sleeping bag: my tent jolted as a body tripped over one of the guy ropes. Our tents were next to the girls with the rodent T-shirts and it became apparent from the tent zipping and slurred conversation that romance was in the air.

"Are you sure you aren't married?" the female voice enquired. Repeated, but very slurred male denials followed. Then more tent zips, a few squeals... and I lost consciousness.

Sunday, I recall, started with desperate queues for the loo... the pain and discomfort on the faces of those at the end of the line didn't bear contemplation. Then a fry-up; gallons of tea, breaking camp and heading back to the launching spot to reclaim our boats. (The boats had been towed back up the Thames that morning).

I looked around at the state of our party, the word zombie suggested too many functioning mental faculties. Space cadets, staring into the trees. I moved slowly trying to accommodate this mother and father of all hangovers. Unfortunately as Terry pointed out to me and several others who were standing around swaying vacantly, this inertia doesn't actually get the boats loaded on the trailers. Perhaps he said something like, "come on Dan, if you would be so kind as to help us lift the boat on to its trailer I would be eternally grateful".

(No, maybe it wasn't quite phrased like that).

I do remember that the journey back required as much stamina as the race. Frequent stops for black coffee and a stretch. Cupped heads, throwing cold water across the face. Eventually three hours later and we crossed the Tamar.

An early night with such a tired body and mind should result in instant and deep sleep. But of course it wasn't like that... so many thoughts and images crisscrossed the brain. The noise, the colour, the bustle at Ham; the start of the race... Vikings, monks and beavers; the Houses of Parliament, the Eye, Zennor alongside; Greenwich lit up; the relief of the finish; the Dutch, the Welsh; The Royal Oak and the landlord. Then my thoughts lingered on the party, Terry's drinking aid and his response at being asked to try it himself

I slid off into unconsciousness with my face set in a half smile.

Chapter 22
Does Size Matter?

Why have I found it so irksome that on hearing that I am "a gig rower" a number of work colleagues and passing social acquaintances will either ask a question along the lines of: "Aren't you too small to row?"

Or state in a less conciliatory, almost accusatory tone: "Surely you're too small to row!"

(This response, I presume is due to the recent and extensive exposure given to the triumphant British sliding seat crews and to the dimensions of the giants that battle it out at the annual Oxbridge Boat Race).

I used to bristle visibly and reply defensively along the lines that, "gig rowing is more about technique and stamina than brute force" – adding with a final defiant flourish, "that I'll have you know I was once a member of a crew that came 17th in the Newquay Championships".

But why bother? Why give these people the satisfaction? I now just agree with their statement. This tactic is effectively disarming.

"Yes, I'm sure you're right, I'm just too small".

A long pause ensues usually followed by:

"Why do you row then?"

To this I calmly reply that I failed to read the small print of the rowing club entry criteria and before I knew it found myself sitting in a boat surrounded by five James Cracknell look alikes: 6ft 3inch, 15 stone Adonai with washboard stomachs, six-packs and long, bronzed limbs. A pause to take in the wrinkled brow and narrowing eyes.

"However, I was put in the back of the boat, given a special half-size Balsa wood oar and told to keep in time. That was ten years ago. Now all the crews have a white midget at the back, it boosts the morale of the other five and increases spectator interest".

Another pause.

"You're making all this up aren't you?"

Or some ask, "Are you taking the piss?"

What John Cleese once called stating the "bleedin' obvious".

In reality, gigs are not constructed for people of uniform size. It's not the Leander 8 we're talking about – with measured sliding seats. In a pilot gig, the gap between the fixed wooden seats varies. There is far more room to reach the oar forward and back in the middle of the boat (at numbers 3 and 4), than there is in the bow or the stern (1 and 6). The angle of the oar is also shallower on entry to the water, in the middle, explaining the greater length and weight of the 3 (bow-side) and 4 (stroke-side oars).

So those with the long reach and long limbs can row there, while those of us with a more compact physique learn the finer arts at the pointy ends of the boat.

They say that what is important is to pull in excess of your own weight. So if you're weighing the boat down at a lardy 16 stone then you're obligated to pull like **** to justify selection.

Aerobic fitness and good strength/weight ratio wins every time. Well, 'tis true I've got no evidence to support that, but it's the view I'm taking unless I'm subject to a sudden mid-life growing spurt.

Chapter 23
The Press-gang Mentality

For the majority of Pilot Gig clubs, selection is a nightmare. For one thing, it has to happen in multiples of six with no subs allowed half-way through a race. For another, it is hard to establish the sort of meritocracy inherent in a squash ladder or golf handicap.

The end product of the collective effort is what counts, not the strength of any one individual. So aside from being captain, the only way in popular clubs to ensure a place in the boat is to get that 4x4 you have always wanted and attach a tow hitch.

All clubs need selfless folk prepared to get up with the Saturday dawn chorus (as Rab and Jezza are just returning from their parties) and hitch up the trailer. The first task is to arrive at each gig rowing event hours before the start to unload Falcon virtually on your own – other club members always promise to help, but rarely bother to turn up (I know I have been one of them). Then the worst bit, staying on, sober, to the bitter end and having to watch your colleagues throwing down the ale. After this it's time to load her back onto the trailer and drive back to Devoran.

Such people are worth their weight in Doombar bitter but rarely receive such well deserved recompense. In my view, the least they can expect is to choose their spot in the boat, regardless of rowing ability. After all, the six best rowers in the world won't win a lot without a boat.

Recently one of our major towers fell and broke his ankle. The sympathy for his personal suffering came later. The first response I heard was, "Oh God, Jase, how could you do that? Now, how are we going to get the boat to St Mawes!" It reminded me of one of those early racist Tarzan films where a native porter falls off a mountain path and the white expedition leader groans, "Oh God, there goes our salt supplies". During the hospital visit, as Jase, still in obvious pain, lay sweating on his bed, Brian decided to ask him a question.

"Now, Jase, since you were reckless enough to do this to yourself and can't drive any more, I don't suppose there would be any chance of us borrowing your new Range Rover?" A stunned silence ensued as heads were slowly shaken and eyes diverted to the floor.

"Look mate," continued Brian, "not all the time you understand, only on a Saturday".

That's it Brian, pick up the shovel and keep digging.

Occasionally at Devoran PGC there has been a selection issue about who should row in which crew. More often than not, with regard to the men, this involves B crew rowers complaining that someone is trying to put them in the A crew. In response to one of the women asking why it mattered, after all the course was the same for everyone, Andrew replied, that, "yeah, that's true, but it's more serious in the A's isn't it? So it matters more when you lose".

(Is this the attitude that built the Empire, I ask myself?)

Being short of rowers also puts you on the spot to row twice. No problem for young, fit members like Adam, but on a hot day or in rough seas not always my idea of fun. Someone is missing the point here, the place to head for after you have rowed is the bar, not another seat in the boat. Still, you help out if you have to. It's better to be needed than ignored. I hear that the time comes to aging rowers in the bigger clubs when requests for their rowing prowess rapidly diminishes.

As the youngsters start taking their place, the writing for the gnarled veteran can appear to be on the wall. Then what do they do? Well, in a few cases migrate to Devoran. We are an inclusive church and there is usually a place in our B crew for the aging refugee. As for Devoran's own veterans? It may be increasingly painful and the swirls coming off your oar may diminish with the passing of the years, but what would Saturdays be like without the colour, bustle and occasion of another event?

The anticipation of the race; the tension on the start-lines; the adrenaline rush; the effort, the sweat; the craic and the beer. So we never turn down a seat in the boat. You never know when it might be your last opportunity and as the saying goes "you are a long time retired".

But the need for young blood is as pressing as ever.

Lord Nelson had it easy, didn't he? His heavy mob were released into the port towns such as King's Lynn and Falmouth with the authority to press-gang into the Navy young men whose only intention when they left home that evening would have been to have a sociable beer with their mates. Terry has contemplated such an approach, but the worry is that if we forcibly kidnap rowers they might subsequently turn sulky and be reluctant to stand their own round in the bar. So we are still left with word of mouth persuasion and recruitment drives.

I think of the word of mouth thing in terms of evangelical religion. I would be tempted to follow only a spiritual leader who lived his life demonstrating the virtues of his faith… on the basis that, maybe if I believed in those same principles I could acquire that degree of serenity. So, I sometimes wonder if I am the person to be proclaiming the publicly perceived virtues of rowing. Strength, fitness, discipline and adherence to the healthy lifestyle… training as the sun rises and back for a bowl of muesli and a plate of free-range eggs.

"Honestly mate it's really good for you", is a message best given by those who are living proof of its veracity. The problem is, we lack sufficient numbers of such missionaries. So some of the younger male members, such as Rab and Paul, decided to take over the recruitment drive. The first phase was to target the predominantly young female students migrating in for the start of the Autumn term at Falmouth Art College. Posters were circulated and a Sunday afternoon minibus was organised to Devoran quay.

Now this sounds so club spirited and altruistic… to be prepared to give up hours of one's time to training others in the finer techniques of sea rowing, but I sensed a whiff of ulterior motive. Was this really just a master plan to create a pool of on tap female talent for Rab and Paul's subsequent entertainment and coupling ambitions? (I've heard their conversations in the pub). Well, whatever the intentions, the strong-limbed young women we recruited last year have proved more than able to resist uninvited amorous offers from and their rowing has come on a treat.

Others, 'tis true, may have chosen to be more accommodating, but in some cases this can also be helpful in prolonging their involvement with the club. Strangely, not many men have come through this route – possibly none – so as the female numbers gradually increase (albeit with students on fixed term courses) Devoran PGC's male rowing population is staying pretty static and woefully inadequate.

To be fair, I have noticed that an additional problem with male recruitment is that when you can persuade a friend to come and try it, the vast majority never return. In the past, I have arranged for several very fit squash players to turn out on a Sunday morning and come for a 'trial'. We have always treated them well and tried to be encouraging and they generally get out off the boat claiming to have enjoyed the experience. But they still don't come back!

The reason for this, I believe is that the gig rowing technique is not something you can pick up instantly and males often feel self-conscious if they can't get it right the first time and don't like to be seen to fail. However much you explain that in a few weeks they will be getting the hang of it, the next Sunday it is back to the core members again. Perhaps we will soon be driven to bribery... a free rowing vest and a pint of Doombar to any returning rower. The difference seems to be that the women don't seem to mind learning and persevering. They are essentially less vain and less self-conscious. What you don't point out at this stage is that gig rowing is an incredibly time-consuming sport and that if you wish to keep in touch with your family or do anything useful at home it's a no no. That suits me, but I am obviously a dying breed...

Based on our experiences, perhaps Nelson should have advertised his job vacancies to women; then he wouldn't have needed those press-gangs.

Chapter 24
Helford and the Hooray Henries

Points of Interest

Helford River Gig Club was founded by a small group of spouses in the Prince of Wales pub, Newtown, St Martin, on August Bank holiday 1993. Each person donated £5.00 as a down payment on the grand project.

The first gig, Helford, was built by Ralph Bird at Devoran and launched in August 1995. A second gig, Golden Gear, funded by a Foundation grant from the Sports Council, was launched at the World Championships in May 1998.

By September 1999, the men's and women's A crews were finishing in the top ten at the Newquay County Championships as the club went from strength to strength. The next step was to acquire a permanent gig shed which led to the purchase and adaption of Gweek Sports and Social Club. A third gig, Merthan, was built by D and J Currah of Looe in February 2000.

The Helford Estuary, one of the most beautiful in Cornwall, is famed for its crystal clear water, oyster beds, oak-wooded banks and the partially thatched village of Helford.

Just west of this picturesque village is Frenchman's Creek, an inlet immortalised by Daphne du Maurier in her novel of the same name. From the mouth of the river, between the two imposing headlands, to the intriguingly named village of Gweek, the Helford follows a winding path of approximately seven miles. This is now the established course for the River Race organised on an annual basis by Helford River Gig Club.

The crews congregate at Helford Passage on the eastern side of the estuary opposite the village of Helford. The gigs are then unloaded from of their trailers and onto the beach in front of the Ferry Boat Inn. ("A hostelry of character", so sayeth the guide book).

This is a Shangri-La setting for a gig club, especially one with Devoran's insatiable thirst. But it's unnerving and unhelpful having the ultimate goal so close to the start. This can sap the will and lead to your potential crew suddenly finding reasons why they shouldn't row and why "so and so" would be better taking their place. You know the sort of thing, "The shrapnel wound's playing up again so I'd better wait in the sun outside the pub and prop the leg up on the table".

Far better to have the pub at the end of the race. Getting this lot into the boats and out to the start-line given this distraction is like tearing children from the comforting arms of their mothers on the first day at school.

The summer clientele of the Ferry Boat is certainly different in nature to the locals to be found in the majority of pubs frequented by gig rowers. This is the domain of the Hooray Henries, the Hampstead-on-Sea set. Groups of excitable youths sit in the sun with their Pimms, their well-modulated vowels prominent as they exchange data on the size of Daddy's yacht and the various merits of exclusive French ski resorts.

The surrounding small lanes are being overrun by Volvos and top of the range 4x4s and the beach is milling with manicured Labradors and elegant Afghan hounds.

To return to the race. Prior to assembling at the start-line, logistics demand that at least half the cars are left at Gweek. To enable us to get back, Terry's big open-backed truck comes in useful as he can follow our cars down to Gweek and then put all the crew in the back and retrace the journey to the Ferry Boat. This is an interesting experience as Terry drives his truck twice as fast as I drive a car.

We hang on for dear life as we are swung round one hairpin bend after another until our grips are inevitably loosened and we fly across the metal floor. Think pinballs in a scene from *Tommy*. After this experience I can't understand how those Sudanese guerrilla types manage to terrorise anyone from the back of moving vehicles. If I had charge of a Gatling gun, after a few miles of Terry's driving I'd be so disorientated I'd be more likely to shoot my fellow passengers than any passing villagers.

Rowing out to the mouth of the Helford river to the start 'line' is one of the more memorable rowing experiences. This really is a beautiful, unspoilt estuary with the National Trust hamlet of Durgan flanked by the two exquisite sub-tropical gardens of Trebah and Glendurgan. Across the water on the southern side are Frenchman's Creek and other sandy coves to the east.

In 2005, however, after we had rowed out into the choppier water, the start was postponed due to the predicted late arrival of the Falmouth gig. (I believe the trailer had got a puncture on the way down the hill). The low boredom threshold of the two Devoran crews was quickly apparent and we were soon splashing each other with water off our paddles as the other crews floated quietly by and tried to focus their minds on the demands of the gruelling race to come.

After about half-an-hour Nikki pushed past me. She was clambering down the boat holding a bucket and when she reached the stern she announced, "I've got to go... so, well you can look this way if you really want to, but don't say you haven't been warned". The boat went quiet accentuating the rattling of pressurised liquid into a bucket. She then had a "brainwave". This involved a request for Lucozade and a direction for Claire, our cox, to get right up close to the other boat. As we did this Nikki stood up, picked up the bucket and hurled the yellow contents across the heads of Sharon and Sue in Fear Not. Now these two, like all the crew in Fear Not, had been well aware of Nikki's bladder movement and, in fact, had been loudly commenting on the process in less than supportive terms.

"Aagh, oh God, 'ick... ", shrieking and screaming followed Nikki's freely given shower and two of the crew nearly fell in the water.

"God, that's disgusting", squawked Sharon, a hygienist by occupation and a newly-recruited, rather prudish individual. "Uuh, uuh". Nikki left them to marinate for a minute or so longer before giving the game away.

"It's only sea water with a squirt of Lucozade you dunces. I washed the bucket out the other side of the boat. Honestly, you lot, what a performance over half a bucket of salt water!"

The race eventually started an hour late, Irene, the Falmouth gig, turning up to an ironic cheer. There is no doubt if I'd known now what an awful experience it was going to be I would have feigned a sprained ankle and stayed in the Ferry Boat. We had a crew which included four veterans and two virtual novices. Not the best combination for a seven mile row.

The main problem, however, was Claire, our novice cox. A large, assertive woman, with a background as a nightclub bouncer, Claire had only one gear to her coxing. This was foot on the floor, flat out. There was to be no settling into a steady rhythm, no nurturing the novices. It was full on, in your face crew flogging.

Within the first ten minutes we had been repeatedly called, "up for ten", and commanded to, "drive it on harder and burst our bollocks". The other boats had pulled calmly away with long, slow, clean strokes and we were left thrashing down through the water like a dyspraxic water beetle.

Claire must have been watching that Charlton Heston movie about Roman galley slaves. We were being verbally thrashed and common sense had long taken a back seat. I tried to gasp a few comments to the effect that we were burning ourselves out, but for all the good it did I might as well have been trying to pass an Amnesty International petition to an Inca chief.

"More effort… I want to see more pain on your faces, another ten… "

I gave up trying to be heard and just tried to block out the noise and slow the stroke down. By now the novices were hardly getting the oar in the water and the other boats were out of sight. If I could have summoned the energy I might have attempted a Fletcher Christian like mutiny and tipped Claire over the side.

Eventually we did finish and six bodies collapsed on the shore at Gweek immediately adjacent to the Seal Sanctuary sign. I recall thinking that I needed sanctuary more than the bloody seals... as for Claire, bless her, my idea of a keel-hauling was overruled.

That race cost us two rowers as neither novice returned... they probably moved on to less demanding activities such as single-handed ocean rowing or serial triathlons.

Chapter 25
The Art of Coxing

Over the years, I have learned that there is more to coxing than pointing the boat at the first mark and picking up a metaphorical bullwhip. Tides, currents and winds play a pivotal role and the effective cox knows how to best exploit the relationship between them. Unfortunately, not everyone manages to acquire these skills.

Some years ago, during the Truro River race, the Truro boat was seen to take the wrong fork up the estuary. Witnesses still repeat the story with incredulity. It occurred with a novice cox who did not know the water (although you wouldn't think it was difficult to follow the course of the river into the Carrick Roads). Jack, a recent arrival from London, had volunteered for the job as his wife was rowing her first race. But being an inexperienced crew, no one spotted the fact that, into the wind and head bowed, he had departed up a tributary.

Eventually, the water course narrowed as the mud increased and the first voices were raised questioning his navigation.

When the mistake became obvious, the comments from the crew were not primarily of the, "Oh, Jack, easily done mate, we do sympathise" variety. They were delivered in what is often described as industrial or colourful language. In a manner that in political speak would be reported as robust.

The approach and psychology of Coxwains varies enormously. For example, there are the screamers, the cajolers, the enforcers/bullies and the cool cats.

During the London River Race, a neighbouring club's cox started screaming at her crew before they had even reached the start-line. This was Alex Ferguson hairdryer stuff. It was embarrassing to watch and must have been exhausting for the recipients.

Many rowers leave the house to get away from domestic verbals, and want the decibels turned down in the boat. But believe me, the naggers and verbal floggers have infiltrated at every level. The constant calls of, "come on, more effort! You can do better than this" echo around the Carrick Roads.

Under such an onslaught, you stagger out of the boat, self-esteem around your ankles, convinced that you are the worst gig rower on God's earth. After one such row, I said to the cox in question, "thanks Pat, I feel great. Just get me one of those pointy hats and I will pull on the club hairshirt, and stand in the corner of the pub and face the wall". You dread the next practice as the nagging will start again. "Come on Dan, lean back, hands forward first… when will you ever learn?"

It's no good protesting that as you have only been in the boat for about ten seconds you are just beginning to re-orientate yourself from the effects of a horrendous day at work.

"Bring the oar out square; push it longer; lean back straight; head up; use those legs. For God's sake my mother could do better than… "

I wake up screaming... Anne is there to comfort me. "It's all right dear; you were having one of your 'Felicity coxing you' dreams again. Just close your eyes and think of the nice girls in the Salcombe calendar".

Then there are the motivational coxes... positive people with big hearts, who pour praise on your every move. When Frank coxed us it was all, "brilliant rowing boys, absolutely brilliant boys, she is absolutely flying". Then out of the corner of my eye, I would see another boat go past.

Then Frank's voice again, "fantastic, that's doing it boys, great stuff... keep in there". I am now thinking to myself, "yes Frank; I would love to believe you... but if we're rowing so incredibly then what superlatives could you possibly find to describe those ten other bloody crews that have just pissed past us?!"

Still, this approach is marginally better than the non-communicating cox, who sits there happily daydreaming and leaves his or her crew to motivate themselves.

During one race, I was subjected to this treatment. Halfway to the second mark, during a particularly peaceful interlude, when all that could be heard was the gentle lapping of the oars, I shouted, "for ****'* sake Graham, *say something*!" Graham turned his head in my direction, the hurt reflected in his gentle expression. He replied quietly, "a pleasant afternoon, isn't it Dan? Are you enjoying yourself?"

Needless to say the timing went to pot, heads dropped, and by the time we had finished the race the other gigs were being loaded onto their trailers. Nice guy that you are, Graham, don't call us, we'll call you.

The coxes that do it for me are the born motivators. These people can see and adjust technical faults, but crucially they can make you truly believe in yourself, and inspire you to row for each other. My daughter, Gen, a highly competitive animal, showed a natural aptitude, for this, and would entreat you to, "believe in yourself... take pride in every stroke". She would then ask us to row ten strokes for the person in front of us... "That's it, Dan, do it for Colin, help him out".

And when you did pull harder, and row better as a crew, this could be followed up by justified praise and encouragement. "You've passed Mevagissey, they can't live with you... You are the ones with the pride, the commitment to each other".

In the last leg of the races, the Devoran men are notoriously weak, but when Gen coxed we believed her when she said that, "we were too proud, too supportive of each other's efforts, to let another crew go by". For once we didn't, we held them off, and I came out of the boat feeling that (despite the rumours) I really was a half-decent gig rower.

Apparently, some of the top crews have ice-cool coxes, who never raise their voices... just whisper things like, "you know what you have to do, you do it everyday in training... go now "

This style definitely would not work for Devoran for various and obvious reasons.

As I said, there is more to coxing than psychology and technical input. Most courses are kite shaped, and involve turning three marks.

This means that the cox must get the boat in the optimum position well before the mark to "secure the water". This is achieved when the umpire boats believe that you have the front and inside berth, and therefore asks the rival crews to back off.

This is definitely not as easy as it sounds, and clashes on the marks are regular and sometimes vicious. An example of the polite negotiation that often occurs between coxes as the first mark is approached.

Devoran cox, "for **** sake St Ives, give water".

St Ives cox, "move over yourselves you blind tossers".

And, as the boats clash:

Devoran cox, "for God's sake you imbeciles move your ******* boat out of the way".

At this point, rival crews will sometimes behave like sailors in the Napoleonic Wars. They start to wave the oars down on top of each other and snatch out each others pins (thus preventing the opposition rowing).

Eventually, the boats are untangled and you carry on the best you can until the next mark, when it all happens again.

After one such recent encounter with a crew from Mounts Bay, we had just staggered back onto the beach, licking our wounds, when I noticed an older member of their crew walking over towards us. Mmmmm, I thought, this could be interesting. When he got to within a few feet of me, his face broke into a huge smile. "Wasn't that just brilliant?" he asked. "Just like a gig race ought to be. No quarter asked, none given. More like the good old days. Bash, clash, and wallop, and on we went... "

A pause... "Anyway, I really enjoyed it lads, and look forward to next week. You coming up to the bar, I'm getting them in".

For me, that afternoon epitomised the essence of gig rowing – compete hard, leave it on the water, back to the bar together.

Teaching a new recruit the first principles of coxing can be exhilarating, frustrating, expensive... and funny at times. This is when you find out who doesn't know their left from their right. Who is dyslexic, dyspraxic, dysfunctional, or just plain disengaged from reality. My own experience probably falls into the latter category. I recall taking ages to grasp the cause and effect resulting from a change in rudder direction... the boat always went in the opposite direction to the one I predicted. This resulted in mass panic, raised voices and near misses with 10K yachts.

"Just testing boys," I'd contribute, while sucking on my teeth. It's unfortunate that our boats are generally launched backwards off the end of the slipway. It is particularly difficult having to start off by reversing a boat out of a harbour that is surrounded by an ever increasing flotilla of moored luxury vessels.

The six rowers have to begin by backing up their oars (the opposite action to rowing forwards). In order to turn the boat, you rapidly have to decide which side should stop rowing, and which side should continue to hold water. I used to hope that through the law of averages I'd get this right fifty percent of the time, but no such luck.

Due to my incompetence, the rowers would often end up having to ship oars and lean out of the boat to push the fast approaching yachts and/or the harbour wall away with their bare hands. With spectating fellow club members either laughing or cursing, panic sets in and once clear brain connections start to resemble a plate of spaghetti. This is now 'hole in the ground' territory... and we are on the water!

The problem is there are no dual controls within a

gig, and no precedent to stick L plates on the outside of the bow and the stern. Then there are so many things to consider simultaneously... the timing of the strokes, the balance of the boat, the proximity of others, the state of the water... and then yet one more crucial action to remember... to turn the boat around the marks.

The last novice cox who raced our gig forgot about this last point and careered past the first mark crashing into the two gigs on the outside of her. Mayhem... fearful oaths from Porthleven, and poor Lesley, left with hands across face in panic mode. All part of the learning curve...

Earlier this season, as one new cox started out from the harbour, we soon realised that he had a speech disorder. (A bit like that Shakespearean character who muddled the order of his words). James started off by demanding that we, "stroke up on our backsides"... "I think you mean, 'back up on stroke-side'", I helpfully interjected. But I hope James continues to cox, because he is a great source of entertainment.

Another recent novice cox had heard his more experienced mentors counting tens and tried to emulate this. The problem is there is a method to this procedure. You count as the stroke oar exits the water... so if a cox starts randomly counting it creates chaos. The crew end up whirling their oars around as if wound up like clockwork toys.

The chaos really intensifies when novice coxes are used to cox novice rowers. (Imagine a learner driver teaching six others how to drive). You hear the poor crew members staggering out of the boat, completely confused by a series of conflicting messages.

"Well John told me to lean back".

"No. Lesley definitely said; just pull it to your chest".

"Graham said, we have to keep it long".

"Peter wants it short and punchy".

I dread their entreaty to me to clarify these matters. Immediate prevarication follows. "Well it all depends, I suppose, on the tides, the conditions, the balance of the crew, so I can't exactly say for sure. I'll look into it for you... oh God, is that the time, I must dash I have got an important engagement at 'the Office' ".

Chapter 26

The Newquay County Championships

Points of Interest

Newquay Rowing Club was formed in 1921 and began by acquiring and restoring three local pilot gigs, Newquay, Dove and Treffry. (The Treffry was the pride and joy of her builders, the Peters family, and later became the template for a new generation of gigs).

The Newquay club started to revive a sport that had all but disappeared towards the end of the 19th century with the decline of the gigs as working boats. Their first gig trophy, the Silver Gig Trophy, was introduced in 1922 and is still in existence and awarded after inter-club races.

After the Second World War, rowing as a sport increased in popularity around the Cornish coves, but Newquay continued to be the only club to race gigs, purchasing and then restoring four abandoned boats from the Isles of Scilly. (During the 1960s as gig racing once again caught on in the Isles of Scilly, this process was reversed as the Shah and the Bonnet were returned to the islands).

By the 1980s the popularity of gig rowing was rapidly spreading along the Cornish coastal ports. As a consequence many new gigs were being commissioned and a new generation of boat builders were being inducted.

*The first Newquay men's championship took place in
1979; the ladies' championship followed in 1980, and
finally the junior championship was established in 1988.*

It's teeming with rain and the damp, dank atmosphere
is rich with the sweet smell of diesel and the aroma
of rotting fish. Welcome to the Newquay County Gig
Rowing Championships. A bleak prospect if you are
rowing, but if you are here to hang around supporting
your women's crews it's an even more extreme exercise
in patience and masochism.

The championship is held over the second weekend
of September. The first and second rounds and the
quarter-finals are completed on the Saturday, leaving
the semi-finals and finals to be concluded on the
Sunday. With six races and two heats in each, the first
round lasts all morning. I wander around, grazing
on junk food and watching the resident seals as they
slide languidly through the water. As the rain drives
into the harbour on a strengthening easterly, my newly
acquired waterproof is proving predictably porous.
Hyperthermia beckons as I seek refuge in Newquay
Gig Shed clutching my third cup of stewed tea. (By now
even the alternative plan of re-decorating the bathroom
is increasing in appeal).

Huddling under rapidly erected shelters or
hovering by the edge of the shed, the women patiently
await their heat. Devoran women's A crew is drawn
in heat five. Its 10.00am when race one eventually gets
under way; only another two or three hours and our
girls are on. A few crews start to warm up by running
up and down the hundred or so steps that lead down
to the harbour. Devoran decide to keep their powder

dry; our attitude is that it's easier to put on a coat than to pull cold muscles and end up too knackered to pick up the oar.

The follow boats start to pull up by the harbour wall and I decide to relieve the boredom by climbing aboard. As I do so a lean, fair-haired woman jogs by in a bedraggled state. The writing on the back of her vest entreats the reader to "Kiss my Oars". I recognise the Salcombe colours. Recent recruits from Devon, Salcombe are now established on the gig rowing circuit. Their event last year was particularly memorable for Gemma, one of our ladies' A crew. Walking out to our boat, she fell straight through the rotting pontoon and slid down into the water. Funny for us, (yes, we are all heart) but very painful for Gemma. Lots of nasty scrapes and bruises but, amazingly no broken bones.

Salcombe are an innovative lot and in an effort to raise funds they published the first naturist gig rowing calendar. Nude female rowers (don't blame me if they're sexist) are arranged in various poses, the oars strategically placed to avoid overt embarrassment and possible prosecution. With oars supported between strong thighs (calm down out there), you didn't need to be Dr Sigmund Freud to pick up on a few dodgy innuendos.

As I slip onto the follow boat, I become aware that my fellow travellers are all unfurling fishing rods, and attaching smelly bait to hooks. Yep, my instincts are right. This is the deep sea angling trip. Just time to climb off onto an adjacent vessel and join the gig supporters. The captain is slumped against the wheel and I overhear a couple of his mates discussing their long night out. One of these men unfurls a hat and waves it towards me. "Two pounds a trip, come on let's get Fred some beer money". It looks to me like Fred needs a cup of tea and a cold shower, but I still pay up. Before we leave, I try and engage one of these old Newquay seadogs in an "authentic Cornish conversation".

"How are the herring shoals doing these days? What tonnage are you catching?" Matey raises an eyebrow, "How should I know about that... we bought her last year to take the tourists around the bay, and then to make a few bob from you lot".

The seals have now come right up to the side of the boat. Huge brown heads and shining black eyes survey the scene. They roll on their backs and snort, demanding attention from their captive audience "The tarts," I hear Graham comment. "And look at the size of them... like furry Pavarottis".

"If swimming's so good for you then why are they so fat," I reply.

"It's all down to diet, I expect, they probably live off rejected chips and pasty crusts instead of sand eels".

The bleary-eyed captain has now left the wheel and wandered over. A smaller boat speeds by and this prompts him into conversation. "Bloody hell, he's at it again. That's my son that is, drives my other boat like he drives his Golf GTI. Madness, he'll be into the harbour wall in a minute. Myself, I've got a Mondeo. I show him how to drive smoothly, conserve fuel".

Eventually the boat lurches into life and we are off. It's a pity his son's not driving as we are last out of the harbour and never get near to catching up with the leading gig. Inevitably that leading gig is the Irene Too, rowed by the incomparable Falmouth A crew. Thanks to these girls, suspense is not a concept associated with the eventual outcome. All bets are off with the bookies. (If this was a horse race, a handicap would be imposed along the lines of Falmouth towing the QE2). In dog racing terms, as the action proceeds, it is equivalent to watching a Greyhound being pursued by a pack of Dachshunds. Falmouth are so far ahead, and surrounded by so much empty water, that it's unclear in which race they are actually rowing.

These girls are from another planet, and unless Redgrave, Pinsent and co come out of retirement and dress in drag their progress will be unimpeded. All season, in all conditions, they have comfortably beaten our men's A crew times! On hearing this, Brian, our resident male supremacist, spluttered, "How can they? That's bollocks, we're men".

"Other than being bigger, fitter and technically better than us I can't imagine how they do it," I replied. " Oh and they row as a crew and don't drink ten pints on a Friday night".

To give an example: Judy is 6ft 2ins tall, broad-shouldered, straight-backed and with legs as long as Newquay's flagpole; although more shapely, I concede. When Jude gets out of the gig and rises to her full height, jaws drop open and the sky darkens. In short, a rowing goddess, who intimidates other crews with the magnificence of her physique. (I suppose this must how the early English rugby teams reacted to the emergence from the Twickenham tunnel of the giant, teak-hard All Blacks. Immediate mental capitulation of the it's-not-fair-look-at-the-size-of-them variety). Encouraged by team-mates, Graham later indulged in a desire to touch one of the Falmouth crew to see if they were real. He badly stubbed his finger and the jury is still out.

Before the Devoran girls go out, I wander back around the harbour. A crew row in beneath me, their race completed. I glance at their rowing vests… their club name is followed by the word "women". Noting two giants in the bow, I hope that this labelling policy isn't in anticipation of possible gender confusion.

Devoran A eventually get their turn. They row with good timing and by coming second in a heat of four they progress to the second round. In the second round they are drawn against stronger boats and gradually drop off the pace to come in last. However, once again, the style holds together well and heads don't drop. That's it then for this competition and the girls head for the bar.

Anne, meanwhile, has been out on the follow boats, brandishing her new state-of-the-art camcorder. Is this the sadistic act of a deposed A crew rower or a helpful attempt to collect the data necessary to improve our girls' performances? On the beach afterwards, Anne approaches the exhausted crews. Falmouth eagerly cluster around her, displaying a forensic interest in analysing their perfectly honed technique. Mounts Bay show a healthy curiosity. The Devoran girls, however, seem to be backing away, their body language implying, "Oh my God, Anne's gone on a follow boat and taken a bloody video. The cow". I hear mutters along the lines of, "I just couldn't get comfortable in the boat". "It wasn't my best row, the stretchers kept coming out". Later, I am to be subjected to an evening of video clips. What great entertainment. I didn't want to see the Angelina Jolie film anyway.

After the Saturday racing is completed, we retire to the Newquay Rowing Club bar. There we find our women's crew looking as relaxed and at home as Koalas in a Eucalyptus copse. I watch Mary walk up to the congested bar and note her surprisingly rapid return. Mary unburdens herself of her large round and turns towards me.

"Dan, "she enquires, thumping her glass down on the table. "You watched our race. Why are they better then us?"

"Well, "I replied reluctantly, "I think the key is aggression and commitment. You know how you just approached the bar, pushing to the front of that thirsty throng, elbows out, chin forward, full of resolution and self belief. Well, I think that's the attitude you need to take on the water".

A long pause ensues; Mary shoots me a sideways look before turning to Isabelle and exclaiming, "****, sorry I forgot the pork scratchings".

The weather changes for the Sunday finals. The rollers are now screaming in. The white horses clash like angry mustangs at a rodeo and the follow boats jerk about like teenagers in a moshpit. It's exhilarating to watch and, no-doubt, knackering to row in.

The start offers a rare surprise. Caradon and Mounts Bay women surge away at fifty strokes a minute and, momentarily, Falmouth look vulnerable. Every star wanes eventually, could this be their day? But by the first mark, it's Falmouth nosing ahead. The following crews give water and clash, and the race for first place is as good as over. Falmouth surge forwards, long powerful strokes driving through the surf.

Caradon fall back. The stroke rate off the start has taken its toll. Ten minutes later and Falmouth cross the line first... a fusion of power and grace, strong but seemingly effortless rowing, oars synchronised and in control. The race for second place hots up. With a hundred yards to go Newquay A are a boat length up on Charlestown A. And then a spectacular finale... Charlestown get picked up on a huge wave and surf in, thrown forward past the finish line at such a rate that their oars are redundant.

The screaming from the crew is instinctive and age old Newquay watchers can't recall a finish quite like this. Anne's video whirrs and this time it's a real scoop. Tough on the brave Newquay girls, but great entertainment. Watch out for the original footage on *You've been framed*.

Points of Interest

During the early to mid 1800s, gig rowing at regattas was a popular sport and with increasing prize money at stake it could also be lucrative. For example the Newquay regatta of 1852 awarded the following prize money;

1st – Newquay - £1.00
2nd - Treffry - 15sh
3rd - Dove - 10sh
4th - Girl I like – 5sh

Chapter 27
Bring on the Men

During the week between the Women's County Championships and the start of the men's competition, the Devoran B crew boys decided collectively we'd better do some training. For one thing, participation in the championships would involve at least two rows on the Saturday… either the first and second rounds or the first round followed later by the plate race consisting of the six slowest boats. At least we could be sure that our involvement on God's ordained day of rest would not be necessary.

That would mean making the first twenty-four boats out of seventy-odd and as Terry remarked, "There's more chance of us visiting the moon". A positive lead from the captain! This was an ideal scenario for the mature members of the Devoran B crew; get out on the water; give it our best shot, support the A crew and then a few beers in the club bar followed by considerably more back at 'the Office'.

For Christ's sake think of the alternative… if we were to actually row through to the end it would involve four full-blown competitive rows in two days, followed by a final, presumably organised by the Marquis de Sade, that demands two circuits of the course.

I've seen fit, highly trained rowing athletes convulsing and vomiting at the finish as they are being pulled onto the beach. Bloody hell, that's not sport, that's self inflicted torture.

The Monday before the event an unforeseen problem occurs. We've only five men to make up a B crew. Nigel, bless him, doesn't do Newquay... if I listed the reasons why this decision is sensible it would take several pages, so I'll leave it at "better things to do". Jason has broken his ankle in zillions of places, Paul has thrown his toys out of the pram as he didn't get in the A crew and doesn't want to row with a bunch of beer-sodden, washed-up old tossers. I can't blame him, being a few months short of my own half century I still keep up banter about having to row with geriatric fifty year olds.

I mention our dilemma to the captain of a neighbouring club and an offer is immediately made to loan us Spike, a young man who has just started rowing for them. They have an excess of rowers and as they have only one crew, places are at a premium and only the more experienced get selected. I have a mental image of Spike as thin and waif-like, pale and retiring. The real thing comes as a shock. Spike is six foot tall, square jawed, and built like an England rugby flanker. I can't believe our luck. If this guy knows only the blade end from the handle then he's going to be a bonus. Spike gets in the boat. Looking at him among my colleagues, the cuckoo in the nest analogy comes to mind. I find out he's applied to join the Royal Marines. I immediately regret the facile comment I make along the lines of, "Oh yeah, now I see why you volunteered for this. Being able to put Devoran B crew on your CV should tip the balance".

As we settle in the boat, tightening our cushions and adjusting the pins, Anne, our cox, announces that, "right, as Newquay is next weekend, tonight we are going to row hard for twenty minutes. Then we are going to practice starts and then tossing around the marks". I drop my oar in horror, to comment on this proposed training schedule. "Now look here young lady, you may have had a bad day at work and a stressful week, but don't you think you can go taking your personal problems out on us". I pause, "a better option, allow me to recommend a good counsellor".

"Right," Anne replies, "anymore backchat and we row continuously for half-an-hour. None of you lot are fit enough to row once round a course and on Saturday you'll have to do it two or three times. Eyes down the boat, oars just above the water, and follow the hands in front of you… "

After a lung-bursting session, I staggered out of the boat and asked Spike if he fancied coming for a drink. "Sorry mate," he replied. "I've got to go home, go out for a run, and then I'm down to the pool for lane training". I involuntarily reacted with a four letter word. I'm unsure whether this related to admiration or pity. As for the rest of the crew, it was all we could do to stagger to the bar and, with shaking hands, raise a Doombar to our lips.

On Thursday night, I joined the gathering on the beach and overheard that the A crew had taken a decision to try and stay out of the pubs on Friday night. This was proving a full-on dilemma, as if they were to collectively achieve the previously unthinkable. Years of conditioning would now have to be overcome. My helpful suggestions included; handcuffing themselves to furniture and giving me the key, or orchestrating an act of criminal damage to ensure a night spent at her Majesty's pleasure. The final plan? A crew visit to the cinema. Now initially this sounded a good solution... simple and effective, but there could be pitfalls. What if the film finished at 10.15pm? Total horror; imagine coming out into the town and having to pass those familiar bars with forty-five minutes of opening time left. A potential disaster, just a quick one (can't do any harm) could end up in a round each and pints lined up on the bar for last orders. The other problem with this approach to abstinence is psychological. The more you concentrate on not doing something the more it moves to the forefront of your mind. "Just don't talk about it," pleaded Jerry, in an attitude reminiscent of that Basil Fawlty sketch involving German guests and the subject of the war.

Come Friday night and I did wonder at the outcome of their ambitious plan as I wandered down to the Old Quay Inn to have a few relaxing, carb-rich beers with my B crew colleagues.

Saturday morning and an early start. As far as I'm concerned a seriously unfortunate juxtaposition of events. As usual, pitifully inadequate preparation, as I have time to gulp down only half a bowl of cereal. Half-an-hour later and we are driving around Newquay streets trying to find a parking space. We give up and pay the £4 like everybody else.

I'm standing on the harbour and as our heat approaches my bowels go through a familiar routine. The first impulse is that I must get to the loo as a prelude to substantial action. I get within ten yards of the queue for the harbour toilets. 'Basic' is a quite inadequate description, (think '70s Marrakech). The smell could down a rhino at twenty yards. So maybe not. I change my mind for five buttock clutching minutes before attempting a tentative return. Too late, the tannoy crackles into action and our crew is called into the boat. Fumbling with kit... tie in the seats, get the pins, adjust the stretchers. Spike asked if I could reach down and use a short piece of rope to tie his feet in. No-one who knew me would make this request. I've already put on my own cushion backwards and upside down. Too polite to refuse, I bend down and fiddle with the string. It falls straight back off the stretcher. I hear Anne's voice as cox, "Come on, we're last off the beach again... back up together and let's take her out". Spike seems to have got the picture and is tying his own feet in. As we row out of the harbour we hear vociferous support. "GO DE-VO-RAN". Spike also seems to have a private female fan club, and gets his own rousing cheer as we approach the harbour entrance.

It proved an unusual championship. Although we raced twice and came last on both occasions, we thought we had done pretty well – there's more to this than deluded Devoran logic. The boats are evaluated on comparative times, and in both our heats we were drawn against very strong crews. As a consequence our time for the course actually proved quicker than twenty-two other crews. That's twenty-two other crews that had presumably trained and prepared and given it their best shot. I know I'm getting carried away and yes, all right, Falmouth third team were forty seconds quicker. But I think it's a cause for celebration, and I recommend that we drink a pint for every crew we've beaten.

The alcohol-free A crew (plan B was a success) start slowly, only twenty seconds up on our time after the first round. They are not happy with that and as the second round approaches, I sense a steely determination to put the record straight. I put it down to delirium tremens and recommend a pint each... advice that's ignored.

Soon they are gliding out again in their skin hugging, shiny blue Lycra shirts. As the starter remarks to me "It's a pity it's not a competition for the best dressed". The race is off and they produce a gutsy performance, coming third behind strong crews but finishing only a length down. Now it's the interminable waiting around for the results and times of each heat. The prize for the quickest twenty-four is a place in tomorrow's quarter-finals.

This is now a dilemma for the A crew boys. We are sat in the bar, beer and banter flowing, our participation ended. They are all desperate for a drink... no let's think in the plural, and have plans for a good club night out! Yet pride demands aspiring to a quarter-final place and a restless night. The final outcome? They miss out by three seconds. Twenty-fifth place out of seventy and the Rock crew sneak in before them. As the final announcement is made there are conflicting emotions; disappointment, commiseration and relief. But in no time the beer's flowing and they are celebrating a near miss and a substantial improvement on last year.

This time, I didn't get to return to Newquay to watch the final. You guessed it, too many jobs to do around the house. *Hangover, what bloody hangover?*

The final result; Caradon from Saltash secured the title for the ninth time in a decade with Falmouth runners-up.

Caradon are to gig rowing what Doombar is to beer, offering consistent quality, a smooth passage and always excelling in the final round. Always generous with their time and advice, if their domination (like Falmouth women's) has ruined the outcome uncertainty factor, it is up to others to step up to the mark and match their levels of physical and mental preparation.

So come on lads, empty the bloody bar and get on with it.

Points of Interest

In 1956 and 1957 a sliding seat crew from Cambridge borrowed a gig and entered the Newquay regatta. Thankfully for local pride, they failed to beat the Cornish crews. However, given a few weeks tuition on gig rowing technique who knows what the outcome might then have been!

Chapter 28

Weymouth and Pasties the Size of Brian's feet

In mid-October, Devoran Pilot Gig Club returned to Weymouth for a second time. (A historical analogy might be the Vikings returning to Lindisfarne for a another tussle with the monks). I have reason to believe that Weymouth Pilot Gig Club posted scouts on every entrance into the town to give the local residents time to prepare for our invasion... children to the cellars, board up the windows... that sort of thing.

An advance party, Terry, Nikki and close entourage arrived on Friday to prepare the ground for Saturday's grand challenge. The plan being to lay to waste vital elements of the opposition through an extended evening pub crawl.

Anne and I drove up on Saturday morning to find the Weymouth members already in their boat shed, awaiting the arrival of Fear Not and its motley crew. (Terry had to drive the trailer around to the harbour for launching before our lot could row her up). The Weymouth crews appeared to be decked out in war paint – stripes of red, yellow and green, their club colours, covering faces, knees, calves and other areas of exposed flesh.

At the entrance to the Weymouth Gig Shed was a metal plate with the words 'The Darling Arms' embossed on it. Inside, their members were sitting around tables spread with smart tablecloths on which were placed flowers in glass vases. At the far end of the shed, in front of the temporary bar, was a sign announcing 'The Traditional Cornish Wine Bar'. This was Weymouth's way, bless them, of trying to make us feel at home.

The reason for this effort on Devoran's behalf? A month or so previously, our local pub/office, the Old Quay Inn had changed hands. The new tenants who also own several city wine bars decided to give the old interior a makeover. The fireplace came out; the carpet was replaced with burnished wood floors and the interior painted white – including the original black beams. A lot of effort and money went into this 'upgrade', but as you can imagine it was a culture shock to locals and rowers alike.

The new landlady, poor soul, had to deal with initial scepticism at the appropriateness of this new refurbishment (in one case suggestions were made as to where the white paint might have alternatively been put). But Tamsin handled this with good grace and equanimity.

As is her way, Tamsin tends to greet her customers with a cheery "hello darlin'". Hence the inspiration for the name nailed above Weymouth's gig shed. On the outside of the shed to welcome their Cornish guests, Weymouth had stretched a huge banner in Devoran colours with our logo embroidered on it.

The shed was full of beer and Cornish pasties and the sun was shining. Even Ethelred the Unready never got a reception like this. As Anne and I continued to wait for the main body of our crew to emerge, one of Weymouth's bleary-eyed men folk suggested that perhaps, after the excessive indulgence of the night before, Terry and friends might be too hungover to make the water. I gave that idea short shrift. For one thing, to get a raging hangover you have to leave time to let some alcohol leave your bloodstream.

"Believe me; they were just warming up for tonight".

Moments later Fear Not came into view, an unusual sight decked out in green, yellow and red balloons (do you think the Vikings ever thought of that?)

So let the action commence. Well, it doesn't quite happen like that in gig rowing. It's what I call the Buddhist monk mentality. Gig time is relative and patience and forbearance are virtues to be mastered. No action should occur in haste.

The good news was that the sun was still shining. The less good news, it was blowing a 'hooley', a force 6 to 7 north easterly, straight into the harbour entrance. The sea was as disturbed as a Strangeways lifer. The white horses were jostling for prominence. (It would have taken more than Robert Redford to calm down this lot). John, one of their more experienced rowers, glanced towards the harbour entrance and said, "It's only really dodgy when it's breaking against the side wall".

"Like that, and that, and that," I said, following his line of vision.

"Oh, yes," he replied. "I hadn't noticed how bad it had got".

Well, it was decided that the girls would be given the privilege of the first row. I presume this was on a 'we will see what happens to them first, basis'. As we walked out to the end of the quay to watch them rowing out, one of the Weymouth men remarked, "Well, if the boats do come back, I'm bloody well shortening the course for us".

By this time the race had started, and the boats were rearing out of the water like cornered mustangs. Crashing down into the troughs, lurching and weaving like punch-drunk boxers on the verge of a knock-out blow. It was terrifying to watch and as I remarked to Colin, "Bloody hell, my wife is out there. If I'd known it was going to be that bad, I'd have got her to stack the deep freeze with ready-made meals".

I then overheard on a mobile 'phone behind me, a tourist phoning home. He was shouting, "I am on Weymouth quay watching some nutters rowing wooden boats out into a raging headwind. They are either suicidal or completely bloody bonkers!" I wandered on, not wishing to eavesdrop further.

Nearly fifteen minutes had passed and the three boats were still bobbing in and out of view, and heading directly out into the sea. The crunch point would be turning the buoy, the boat having to go sideways on to the sea. About thirty more strokes to go; either they would get around it or there would be some spectacular Sunday morning headlines. Much speculation by the men around me, too close to call. It was too far out for me to see, but I heard the conformation, "Fear Not is around it and heading back".

Huge relief... won't have to console the dog and engage in the mysteries of the washing machine.

Fear Not is now in second place, good effort girls. This prompts realisation of, "Oh God, now it's my turn". Time to head up the 100 steps to the nearest loo. I wonder will I be missed if I lock myself in?

A lung-bursting, arm-wrenching, spectacularly wet

half-an-hour later, and it's time to wrap a shaky hand around a can of the free Bass. Apparently, in common with our crew, it is well past the sell-by date. I could only make out an -04, but at that moment, I wouldn't have cared if it had been 1804.

Pasties then appeared, huge things, the size of Brian's size 14 feet... I am not in a position to comment on the comparative taste... but yeah, like you, my instinct goes with the pasty.

So to the award ceremony. This time Weymouth who had made the first prize, decided that it would be awarded to their triumphant ladies' crew. Their chairman solemnly presented Caz with a mounted golden gig pin.

"Have you got the batteries for it Caz?" shouted Terry bringing down the tone and the house. The main thing is, by splitting the two Weymouth men's crews, we kept our massive 'Weymouth/Devoran Nearly First Trophy', and to a rousing chorus of "it's coming home, it's coming home, it's coming..." we graciously received it. Now it was Terry and Nikki's turn to hand out some well-thought-out gifts. Ominously, Nikki started by saying, "As I know you have a sense of humour... "

Followed by, "For the relief of all those sweaty girls in the boat... "

A large penis lookalike water bottle was unfurled... "squeeze hard and your thirst will be quenched". OK Nikki, let's move on.

But not to be sexist, the men were presented with their own breast-shaped water bottles... never mind mother's milk, these were especially adapted to take Doombar bitter.

After the presentation, my attention was drawn to a notice on the side of their gig shed. It said, "for the attention of naturist rowers". The first paragraph explained that rowing in the buff was nothing to be ashamed of, making reference to an ancient charter of 1756 (or thereabouts) allowing Weymouth ferryman to disrobe at certain times of the day during months containing the letter 'r'.

The notice went on to make reference to rubbed up members, well hard boys, an indignant Nun, and much more besides. (For more details, or the full engaging text, mail Weymouth gig club enclosing a large stamped addressed envelope).

Anne and I left the gig shed soon after the presentation. I had some very specific shopping to do on the way back to the guest house. The next Saturday I was due to attend a special Nelson celebration dinner, and needed to complete my costume by finding a white cravat and thin black cotton or lace scarf. Now to be honest, this is a pretty strange thing to be asking for – either in the women's departments or a gentlemen's tailors – when you are dressed in shorts and a sweaty rowing vest.

In fact, I got some bloody funny looks. The replies from the shop assistants seemed to take ages before the words, "Oh... I see" emerged. Anyway, after an hour of fruitless endeavour, a successful outcome in Claire's Accessories was achieved. I rushed up to the counter, gasping, "fantastic, this is just what I wanted", as I threw down the frilly scarf and black neck band.

"Oh, I see". I noticed the girl's hand hovering over the emergency button.

The plan was for our club members to gather in

the guest house bar at 7.00pm, to prepare to meet our Weymouth hosts in the Jolly Sailor around 8.30pm. Well, it is said you should always warm up before an event. (Having finished putting the boats away, Terry and co had already had a few pints in the King's Arms on the way back). Firstly, we were to rehearse a song, to which Nikki, the club lyricist, had written the words that very morning. This was to be sung to our hosts in recognition of their hospitality. Emily circulated some hand-written copies. As she gave one to Terry he passed wind.

"That's great," said Emily. "I write out all this and you fart at me".

Quick as a flash Colin intervened.

"It's the primitive reaction of a primitive being".

Terry then explained, "Look in Italy it's polite to burp" (is it?). And I have noticed in Weymouth that they show pleasure by farting".

Here is a full version of Nikki's song. Notice the subtle change of words in the final chorus.

"As I looked out once again,
Weymouth still looks the same.
And Mark and Jan are there to greet me.
Down the quay we walk and there sits Penny.
Red, yellow, green – thank God there aren't too many.
It's good to be amongst the friends we know.
And we'll row and drink and all get merry.
Thank God we've got more hair than Terry.
It's good to come and drink with friends we know.
We've come up with just one boat.
The other one she won't float.
But we all still intend to have a good time.
We'll out-row you and out-drink you.

In the Duke of Cornwall we'll out-drink you.
It's good to be amongst the friends we know.
Chorus
As I wake up and look around me,
And there are no boats to see.
And I realise, I realise I'm only dreaming.
The two pin trophy's here to stay.
But it's just on loan till another day.
It's good to be amongst the friends we know.
And we'll row and drink and all get merry.
Thank god we didn't hit your ferry.
It's good to come and drink with friends we know".

Well, we did get to sing it... Terry stopped the band that the pub had engaged for the evening so Devoran could perform some "Cornish words to music". Now I will be honest, we weren't talking the Mevagissey male voice choir here. I never had a clue what the tune was, but at the end there was loud applause and whistles as it seemed to go down well with our generous hosts. As Terry said, "well, we gave it our best shot for you, now let's get back to the beer".

As the evening progressed, it was round to the Cornish Arms for the dancing on the tables. What followed – well, it was not for the blushing violets (I mentioned a watered down version in a previous chapter).

Some of us didn't make the tables, but still perhaps it needed a few introverts to make up the audience and prop up the bar. Well that's my excuse anyway. I think a night club followed...

That night I had a dream... it must have been those cheese and onion crisps. Gig rowing had become an

Olympic sport, and Terry, Nigel, Colin and I were being shown around Weymouth's new Olympic village. Famous rowers and sailors rowed by. "Hi Terry, Hi Dan", came spontaneous greetings from the likes of Ben Ainsley, "Good luck tomorrow, boys, we will be rooting for you. Those Faroe Islands shouldn't be any problem, but watch out for the Dutch".

I remember us unpacking, and then Terry announcing, "Right Dan go and help them bring the Doombar in, this place is like a morgue and we are going to have a party". Nigel and Colin then put up the big Devoran banner, and at the same time the Rum and Shrub Shanty Men (a traditional Cornish Choir) assembled at the back of the gym. Next thing I knew Terry had a loud-hailer in his hand, and was summoning the village folk.

"Right you lot, get down to the gym, *now*. It's party time and Devoran don't take no for an answer".

I recall saying something like, "but Terry, the Olympic finals are tomorrow, this is the culmination of four years of hard training, wouldn't they be better with an early night?". I just recall part of Terry's reply, something about being a boring old fart, before I was being directed to untap the barrels.

The party was a wild success... singing, dancing, and drinking, until the early hours.

And the next day on the water? A clean sweep of the golds. Everyone who had been at the party was stood there on the podium, a medal around their neck... and there in the centre was Terry, a garland on his bald head, gold medal gleaming in the sun. With a wide smile, he turned to me, "tonight is going to be a real cracker Dan, I hope you are up for it?"

I woke up with a start, just conscious of the sound of shouting and arguing below our window, I reached for the water, my mouth feeling like the unmentionable part of a camel's anatomy in a sandstorm.

The next morning at breakfast, amnesia was the order of the day, especially from those female rowers who a few hours before had looked like they were auditioning for the part of Demi Moore in that *Striptease* film (or so Colin told me).

A bracing walk on the beach was required… and then time to withdraw. To wave goodbye to Weymouth once again, to leave it to 'normal' tourists, to allow the pubs to return to their regular rhythm, to piped music and amiable chatter.

Points of Interest

West Dorset has long inspired poets, Thomas Hardy and Williams Barnes to name but two. Try this one in your best Dorset accent:

In Praise of Dorset
"We Do'set, though we mid be hwomely,
Be'nt asheamed to own our pleace;
An' we've zome women not uncomely;
Nor asheamed to show their feace;
We've a mead or two wo'th mowen,
We've a ox or two wo'th showen,
In the village,
At the tillage.
Come along an' you shall vind
That Do'set men don't sheame their kind.
Friend an' wife,
Fathers, mothers, sisters, brothers,
Happy, happy, be their life!

Vor Do'set dear,
Then gi'e woone cheer;
D'ye hear? woone cheer!"
William Barnes

The Weymouth website gives many fine examples of how local club members have carried this proud tradition into the 21st Century. I quote one of my favourites:

An unscrupulous rower from Dart,
Thought rowing more science than art,
Before every race, he'd stuff beans in his face,
And would win with the help of a fart.

Chapter 29
Dinner, Dancing and Cross Dressing

The Cornish Pilot Gig Association Annual Dinner and Dance is the gig rowers' review of the season, an award ceremony, a mega-nosh, an even more mega-piss-up and a chance to find that perfect partner on the dance floor (and then throw up over them?). The venue, a spatial, rather than palatial, Newquay hotel. This could be due to the post-war pivotal role of the Newquay Rowing Club in reviving our sport or it could be due to this garish resort's abundance of cavernous, half-empty hotels prepared to accommodate a gathering that is definitely not for the squeamish.

This is treated as a formal occasion, so it's time to dust off the DJs and rummage through the recesses of the wardrobe for that lime green dress and those trendy knee-high boots (as for the women rowers, we'll come to them later). As I arrive in my pinstripe wedding suit, it's reassuring to see that I'm not the only one sucking in my cheeks and clenching my stomach muscles. To breathe out would be to risk the sound of ripping stitches and invite the feeling of compacted flesh rolling like a small mountain range over the top of my trousers. I console myself with the thought that I must have filled out after all those years of energetic rowing, increased shoulder width, greater bone density, that sort of thing. But even so I've never been able to see why jackets have a bottom button. This only serves to constrict the Devoran gig rower's storage tank of Doombar bitter, the carb reservoir to call on when times get tough. This is nothing to be ashamed of, in fact a common mammalian feature, think repositioned camel hump.

Still it's an incongruous sight, hundreds of burly gig rowers dressed as if they are out for a night at the opera (think Penguins about to explode). I remarked to Terry that it reminds me of those old PG Tips adverts, when docile chimps dressed in frocks and braces sipped tea from china cups. Then I find I'm having to defend the remark, "no Keith, don't get offended just because tufts of hair grow out of your arms and back, it wasn't meant personally".

A figure in a long, glitzy, satin dress rushes by. I am transfixed, staring in disbelief. It can't be, that's Sandra, the sadistic cox from St Piran, the one who, as we turned the mark at Meva, was shouting all those blood-curdling oaths. This could be the biggest transformation since Liverpool became the European capital of culture. I turn around and think I recognise one of the legends of the Newquay A crew... but shiny dress, coiffured hair, trowels of make-up, siren-red lipstick?! Blimey if she had spotty fur gloves on I could be staring at Cruella de Vil.

Within minutes, everyone is called to sit around their tables and the main business of the evening can begin. As the starters are brought out, the CPGA chairman stands to say a few words, to summarise the season and pay tribute to the umpires, officials and all those in the committee who have freely given of their time. My attention returns to the table. The communal rolls have been demolished, the prawn cocktails wolfed and it's now time for the main course. Nathan, the big lad from Falmouth, piles the food onto his plate into an impressive pyramid shape... the potatoes the building blocks for the main structure. For those of you familiar with Desperate Dan of *The Dandy* the only things that are missing are the cow horns.

Five minutes later and full clearance has been achieved, a truly focused effort from Nathan, in a time that even Fern, our Dachshund, would have struggled to better (probably on account of the fact that she would have been forced to chew a few more times). Nathan then looks up and casts ravenous eyes across the table. In a reflex action I instinctively pull my plate towards me.

His club colleagues come up with a challenge. A waiter is summoned to bring in all the remaining roast spuds from the kitchens and Nathan's plate is refilled. This isn't a meal, it's more of a food mountain, substantial enough to alleviate malnutrition across a major African republic. But the big man is refocused and the world's poor are not at the forefront of his mind. At the end of this gastronomic marathon, Nathan slumps back into his chair, sweat dripping from his face, and emits a belch that rumbles like distant thunder around the walls of the hall. The gravy splattered tie is rapidly removed and the shirt buttons ripped apart.

There's a built-in breather before the crumble, allowing the president of the CPGA to detail the results from the summer's starred events and to begin to hand out the trophies. With all the getting up and down to collect silverware this is indigestion time for Falmouth and Caradon but a process that has never before made any demands on the Devoran constitution. But this year the natural order is being challenged and our B crew are here to collect hard earned individual medallions for achieving THIRD PLACE OVERALL.

I'll explain. It wasn't drugs, unless this was a vintage year for Doombar. This was a year when a group of able and experienced rowers fell out with neighbouring clubs and decided to colonise our own sleepy set up. So for once the A crew were suddenly competitive and the B crew, the old stable core of Devoran stalwarts, had a season long opportunity to "train" and row together.

So, to the generous applause of our peers we beat a path to the front of the hall to collect our bounty. Now, to you this may not be on a par with Olympic Glory; mounting a winners' podium, tears rolling down cheeks as your National Anthem plays. We may not be in for a triumphant homecoming, a ticker-tape reception, the Lord Mayor's banquet: the open-top bus ride and freedom of Devoran may have to be put on hold. But hey, we were proud of our achievement. To use an Aussie phrase "a lot of hard Yakka" had gone into that season. I immediately commissioned Anne to start work on building that long overdue trophy cabinet. The memories flooded back; digging deep in that last leg at Meva to see off Zennor's late surge; cutting fine around that last mark at Charlestown to wrestle the advantage from Gorran; driving across the swell at Falmouth to secure second place behind Par: every week achieving a top half-dozen finish, pasties washed down with hard-earned beers.

The post-meal migration to the dance floor followed the predictable time-honoured sequence. The women first, initially to dance with each other, to be eventually joined by a trail of pint slopping, dishevelled manhood, their early evening brush with etiquette now a distant memory. As the night wore on it became increasingly obvious that we were not witnessing a final audition for *Strictly Come Dancing*. Tim, sweaty bare torso to the fore, was weaving around the sticky wooden floor swinging his shirt around his head. Kevin, who appeared to be using Kate to prop him up, was trying to take his trousers off. This was beginning to remind me of a scene from that Jane Fonda film, *They Shoot Horses Don't They*. The one depicting a depression era dance marathon, the last one standing collecting the prize money.

Due to considerations about travelling and anticipated alcohol intake, many of the rowers had booked into the host hotel, and they hadn't done this in contemplation of a cold, lonely night. So, as the first signs of dawn began to lighten the horizon, the drunken mating rituals intensified (from this point on, any further graphic descriptions would leave me liable for prosecution under the 1968 Indecency Act). Suffice to say, I'm told that the hotel breakfast table is a very lonely place and not somewhere for a young man to be seen if he wished to keep his credibility intact.

The next CPGA dinner and dance switched to St Ives, but did not incorporate the traditional prize giving. This now took place at St Austell Brewery as they had become the sponsors of the year's Starred rowing events (the races that determine the final pecking order of the gig clubs). The three key race events are now being called the Tribute Series after the famous (or infamous) Tribute Bitter.

My informed source from within the Falmouth

club had the privilege of attending both occasions. I understand that the highlights included:

- Karen, Falmouth's middle of the boat legend, using all her guile and lack of guile to ingratiate herself with the star guest Ed Coode, Cornishman and Olympic champion. Her attempt to be photographed interacting with her hero in a variety of poses caused much hilarity to her team-mates and we can only presume, various degrees of pleasure/embarrassment to Mr Coode (sad to recall that I never got that treatment after collecting my third place medallion, but I'm a patient man, Karen).

- The evening's compere initially introduced the said Mr Coode as the current Olympic champion of the coxless pairs, surely a major ground-opening-beneath-one moment, as you all know it was the coxless fours. Still, at least he did make a connection to rowing and didn't introduce him as, say, Cornwall's new, 400 metre hurdles champion.

- Cross-dressing in St Ives. This seems to be becoming a Falmouth speciality. Perhaps all those incredibly fit people are becoming amorphous and indistinguishable. The eyewitness account related how two of the slimmer men's A and women's A rowers disappeared into the loo together, re-emerging minutes later sporting each other's finery. Apparently, the male member, (no double entendres please) was a big hit and kept receiving slaps on the bottom from his increasing fan base. Observations were made as to the professionalism of his makeup skills and the seemingly natural

Marilyn Monroe hip roll. Rumour has it that the male in question was visibly reluctant to return to his boring old shirt and trousers and maybe contemplating a change of name and identity.

- Other minor frolics were inclusive of letting balloons off up skirts, napkin throwing and drawing a large phallus on the window (much amusement when the condensation started to run). The significance of this I will leave to the amateur anthropologists amongst you.

The two presentations at the CPGA were for best kept boat and most improved crew. As at Devoran we treat our boats with the consideration that Ozzie Osborne reserves for Sharon, we would have been spared, on this occasion, the lonely walk to the front. But, perhaps as an ironic gesture it should have gone to the Thames towing firm responsible after last year's event for reducing our beloved boat, Falcon, to matchwood. Most improved crew? Well our men's A crew have definitely made progress. But obviously the democratic process deemed others more worthy. As for "my crew", the men's B crew, if we're to aspire to silverware this year, I fear we need to create a new category. My suggestions include: The Most Resistant to Change Cup; The Crew with the Most Individual Rowing Styles Cup; The Regression Trophy. Think of your own and feel free to send suggestions to Norma, President of the CPGA, Cornwall.

NB: If you consider that any of the last section is factually inaccurate and/or grossly insulting to yourself or your club and you feel the need to seek legal redress, then given enough liquid inducement, I may be persuaded to reveal my source (sorry Claire).

Chapter 30

The Devoran Character and Raising Falcon

I have noticed that Devoran PGC can show a slight inferiority complex. Why is it that other clubs seem to have newer kit, less battered boats and gleaming rust-free trailers? I don't think it helps that our normal training site is often shared by a much posher club with a pristine, varnished boat and smartly painted oars. Their rowers turn out in ironed singlets and fit snugly into their shining Lycra.

After a recent row it did not help our collective paranoia to find their captain's two dogs cocking their legs and relieving themselves all over our boat covers. So was this a physical demonstration of their crew's attitude towards our down-to-earth little village club? Tell me this, did these same dogs ever piss on Falmouth's kit? It could have been chance, but as the saying goes, just because you're paranoid it doesn't mean that they aren't out to get you!

Sunday morning horror

The aftermath of the 2005 Thames river race, added further fuel to our collective persecution complex. The procedure is, that after rowing down the Thames from Richmond to Greenwich, the boats are tied up on floating pontoons from which the organisers arrange for them to be attached together and pulled back up the river by barge to the original launching site. From here, they are collected by the owners on the Sunday morning.

This service is prearranged and prepaid. In recent years, however, in the process of turning the boats back up the river several gigs have been damaged. So, on the Sunday morning it was with some trepidation that Terry and several other club members walked down the slipway to look for Falcon and Fear Not. At this stage, the worst expectation was to find a dent here and there and chipped paintwork.

The sight that greeted them was traumatic. Our beautiful, recently restored and repainted pilot gig Falcon was lying virtually submerged. All the oars and equipment had floated away, and the damage to the thwarts and the planking looked terminal. In stark terms, our newest and principal racing boat had been reduced to the status of sodden kindling.

The horror throughout the club was palpable with feelings of shock, anger and incomprehension that such damage could have been inflicted by those to whom our boat had been entrusted.

The process of redress is underway, and we have now all agreed that this is a test of our collective spirit. We will stand firm as a club and rebuild…

The gig rowing community has already been responsive and supportive with offers of both the loan of a boat and kit. With the men's county championship less than a week away, there was a pervasive spirit of defiance. It would take more than the incompetence of Thames bargemen to break our collective will.

In order to try and raise some funds to cover the considerable cost of rebuilding our boat, the committee had decided to arrange a November gig event at Devoran quay. Around the middle of the month there would be high afternoon tides that would give us time to have four or five races before returning to the beer tent and a barbeque.

We hoped for a good turnout and a profit in the bar. We would then have a raffle, followed by other, more creative, fund-raising events... a tombola perhaps? We would then make the shortfall up the hill for an extended stay in the Old Quay Inn. The entertainment would be provided by the Rum and Shrub Shanty Men. So an evening of Cornish singing, led by one of the very best local choirs.

Saturday dawned and the gods were in benevolent mood. Throughout a day of glorious winter sunshine the racing was keen, but in good spirit and Devoran men's B crew weren't last. Thank you Mylor's Pinnacle, we do appreciate the influx of new clubs. Our trophy presentation was different and well matched to the occasion. Nikki and Terry had used the broken planks of Falcon (the pieces with the lettering on) and made them into picture frames. Inside each, they had slotted a picture of the winning gig, taken moments earlier by our on-the-spot digital photographer. Cool or what?

The refreshment proved just perfect in quality and quantity. The goulash sold out, the chilli con carne was hot in every sense of the word, the soup got supped, and the burgers whistled off the barbeque faster than a Caradon boat off the start-line.

Installed in a central marquee was our guest performer, the incomparable Belfast Busker. Long straggly hair, heavily tattooed and dressed in a threadbare vest, he looks as if he has just emerged from a night in the nearest hedge. An old, battered guitar on his knee, harmonica around his neck, he approaches his task with manic energy, rasping into the microphone with strong, hard Northern Irish vowels to the fore. The lubrication is provided by a conveyor belt of Guinness.

Frenetically paced Irish songs, Celtic ballads and sea shanties predominate with an occasional and rather incongruous rendition of some early Bob Dylan and Donovan. So the music is great, but the banter... well, the Irish just have it don't they? Something about their babies being taken by fairies to kiss the Blarney Stone. The Belfast Busker is a regular Celtic traveller, and when he is in Cornwall we use this as an excuse for a club night out.

As the music and banter move on, you realise that this is no place for those with feminist sympathies. His banter is as politically incorrect as his appearance. A hatred of mother-in-laws and the Child Support Agency is combined with tales of drunken exploits and tales of 'loose' women. So if you are of a sensitive disposition please skip the next few lines.

BB: "you know these Wonderbras the girls wear? Have you ever thought why they're called that? Well, I got to take a girl – who was wearing one – home last week... and when she finally took it off, Christ, then I realised where the name came from... I wondered where her tits had gone".

BB: "I'm sorry I was late for today's gig. I've just rushed over from my mother-in-law's funeral in County Fermanagh. She drowned in a wishing well. Be Jesus, I never knew that they actually worked".

As the light faded everyone mucked in to clear up before we headed up the hill for that traditional Devoran Climax, a night in the Old Quay Inn.

Ten pm in the Old Quay Inn and I'll describe the scene. Surrounded by club members, village mates and rowers and supporters from Zennor and Charlestown, everyone is singing along to the chorus of old traditional sea shanties led by the choir, the one and only Rum and Shrub Shanty Men who have now been joined by their Falmouth equivalent. *South Australia*, *Rio Grande*, and the words of *Trelawney* shake our local to the rafters.

In the next room an Indian wrestling competition is going on in the far corner. This is being dominated by an extremely tough looking female from Charlestown who has progressed from beating the women to throwing out random challenges to the men. Strangely, few seemed too keen to be put down in front of their partners and peers (I'd have liked to have done the business with my right arm, but I'm far too gracious to humiliate the fairer sex.) As Anne had already beaten the said challenger at the final of Gorran's hay bale tossing competition, she also took pity on her.

One of the guys standing near me was visiting from Bristol where, like the majority of England, the only singing in pubs comes out of juke boxes and the entertainment is manufactured. "This is so special, you know," he whispered, visibly moved, as fifty odd people joined in the chorus of South Australia and with two Cornish choirs harmonising together it certainly was. Some of us joined in the verses, some the chorus; others, like Anne, just listened.

As Terry commented, the sense of community we

witnessed that night in the pub, the shared culture and traditions expressed the very heart of what gig rowing is, or should be about. Historically a Cornish sport, based on a great seafaring tradition, community based and practised in some of the most beautiful locations in Britain.

No wonder I feel privileged to have been able to have taken part in it.

As the middle of January approached, the date of the Devoran Pilot Gig Club AGM was once again upon us, and a last minute venue was proving hard to find. The village hall was pre-booked for Salsa dancing; the pub rooms were too small. But miraculously, with thanks to Derek our supportive local vicar, a solution was on hand. I do believe, however, it's unusual to conduct a rowing club AGM sitting in the pews of the local church. Anne and I sat several rows back looking towards the committee members shuffling their papers in front of the altar. As I waited for the action to start, I wondered if we were actually going to sing the hymns that were still displayed on the pillar behind the lectern. And where would the Epiphany come into it?

Colin, the chairman, rose and started his address: "Dearly beloved," he began, before stating in more serious tone that his grandfather had, in fact, been a Methodist minister and wondering aloud at how this esteemed ancestor would have reacted to such a secular gathering in "the house of the Lord" (did I catch a note of trepidation?). By now, my thoughts were taken up with how the captain's factual rowing report might be adapted to more appropriately meet the context. I started scribbling a hellfire sermon along the lines of: "Good folk of Devoran, look ye where the boat of the drunken sinners did come... trailing in behind those God fearing men of Caradon... Brethren, 'tis time to take stock of your lives and seek the path of eternal glory, through abstinence and devotion to the purity of rowing".

Initially, it did look as if Nigel, the first speaker, was getting to his feet to mount the pulpit. Now this didn't seem the most appropriate place to deliver the treasurer's report... but, there again, perhaps it would offer the opportunity to put a more positive view on the gloomy accounts:

"As greed is the most cursed vice, let us rejoice brothers at our newly acquired penniless status, thus leading us nearer to the gates of the Kingdom of Heaven".

The brief meeting certainly passed in a more muted and respectful air, in the absence of the usual uncouth heckling and bawdy comments. Two new captains were duly elected, a young and enthusiastic duo. Are Jezza and Gemma now set to invigorate the sleeping giant that is Devoran gig club? Will the talking turn to action and the latent potential of our expanding membership translate to glory in the water? Will a night on the Doombar have as sinister connotations as the name implies? Will circuit training become compulsory and pasta replace pasties?

Some two hours after the meeting, I put some of these questions to Jezza, but my voice was lost in the noise of the bar and Jezza, thinking I was offering to buy another round, just put his thumb up... so only time will tell.

A pause for reflection. So, how many years of rowing

have I got left? Is it time to book the B&B for The Scillies, prepare for a new season, or will I be consigned to the beach with my binoculars to watch a new generation strutting their stuff? Surely not a relatively young man like myself.

However, this self-perception was soon to be challenged. Recently, I accosted a new young colleague at work to suss out the possibility of gaining a new recruit. I explained what gig rowing entailed, the physical demands it made, the rewards... I awaited a reply. Martin looked me up and down, a slight furrow of the brow, eye contact regained. The tone was disdainful. "So you can do it at any age can you? And you obviously don't have to be very fit".

"Thanks pal, remind me to give you another club's address".

So it seems that despite what we think and feel, age does catch up with us... more grey hairs, less grey matter. But as my father used to say, you're a long time retired son, so God and Jezza willing (sorry to put you second mate) come May I'll see you at the start-line off the St Agnes rocks, and let the first man back get them in.

Epilogue

To finish, I'd like to share an email from our recently appointed Chairperson.

Hi to one and all,
It is with great pride that I write this email, as the new chairman and past captain of what is now officially the best gig club in the Cornwall Pilot Gig Association.
Terry and I attended the AGM of the CPGA this afternoon and for those of you who have not already heard the news (I know the jungle drums are already beating) Devoran Gig Club was awarded the CPGA's chairman's cup presented to the club that in her opinion was outstanding throughout the previous year.
I can hear you all thinking, but we did not win anything and this is quite true but to paraphrase the chairladies' remarks:
"I have thought long and hard about who should be the recipients of the cup this year and the club that I have chosen will not mind me mentioning that they do not often win. This said they do attend the majority of events throughout the year and have to be the most friendly and sociable club of the CPGA.
"Also when they attended the London River Race in September where many boats were damaged theirs certainly came off worse. Many clubs would have let this sink them (excuse the pun) but this club took the opportunity to make this unfortunate incident draw them closer together and make the club bond, if possible, stronger.

Epilogue

"They ran an event to remember to raise some funds and are now well on the way to getting their boat back in the water."

Congratulations to you all, this is most definitely a CLUB cup.

Thanks and let's stay a credit to the association for many years to come.

Love and stuff from Nikki

Other books from SportsBooks

Willie Irvine – Together Again
Willie Irvine with Dave Thomas
The remarkable story of the Burnley and Northern Ireland centre forward who grew up in abject poverty, rose to the heights only to fall into depression after he stopped playing. He also found out some remarkable things about his family while researching the book, chiefly that his parents had never married!
ISBN 1899807 33 0
Price £17.99
Format 155mm x 235mm
Hardback
Pagination 240

Twickenham – the History of the Cathedral of Rugby
Ed Harris
The story of rugby's most famous ground, from its days as a cabbage patch to the multi-million sports arena it is now.
ISBN 1899807 29 2
Price £17.99
Format 155mm x 235mm
Hardback
Pagination 192

Europe United – a History of the European Cup/ Champions League
Andrew Godsell
The European Cup and its successor, the Champions League, was 50 years old in 2005 and this book celebrates

all the great games and characters of the world's greatest
club compeition.
ISBN 1899807 30 6
Price £17.99
Format 189mm x 246mm
Hardback
Pagination 224

Another Bloody Tangle!

Peter Bishop
The author loves fishing, sadly the sport doesn't reciprocate.
Amazingly just before publication, Peter won his first
competition and then when the cup was presented promptly
dropped it. The Liverpool Echo said: "echoes of the black
humour of Alan Bleasedale".
ISBN 1899807 28.4
Price £7.99
Format 129mm x 198mm
Paperback
Pagination 224

The Art of Bradman

Difficult to find a new book about the greatest batsman ever.
But this is unique. A selection of paintings of the great man
from the Bradman Museum at Bowral Oval with text by the
museum's curator.
Leatherbound with gold lettering and red ribbon marker.
ISBN 1899807 32 2
Price £25
Format 210mm x 280mm
Hardback
Pagination 240

Colin Blythe – lament for a legend

Christopher Scoble

Colin Blythe was a giant in the golden age of county cricket before the First World War. He was the most famous England cricketer to be killed in the conflict. This is the first biography of a complex personality, who was one of the first cricketers to challenge the game's rulers, demanding to handle his own financial affairs.

ISBN 1899807 31 4

Price £16.99

Format 154mm x 236mm

Hardback

Pagination 214

Athletics 2006

Editor Peter Matthews

The essential yearbook of the Association of Track & Field Statisticians and has been published every year since 1951. It contains details of the Helsinki World Championships. Previous annuals have been greatly prized by all true followers of the sport. Issues dating back to 1995 are also available.

ISBN 1899807 34 9

Price £17.95

Format 148mm x 210mm

Paperback

Pagination 608

The Rebel – Derek Roche - Irish warrior, British champion

Nigel McDermid

The tale of boxing hero Derek Roche is a journey from an Irish council estate to becoming the first Irishman to win a Lonsdale Belt outright. It also tells of Roche's days as a

doorman in Leeds as he sought to earn a living outside the ring. The Irish Post called it a "modern classic". The Guardian said: "refreshingly honest and... genuinely funny".
ISBN 1899807 25 X
Price £7.99
Format 129mm x 198mm
Paperback
Pagination 240

Are You a Proper Teacher, Sir?

Gary Boothroyd

Twenty-seven years of teaching at an inner city comprehensive school might sound like a life sentence to some, but as Gary Boothroyd found out there was a lot of fun to be had as well. His story encompasses the downright hilarious and the occasional stark tragedy. The Times Educational Supplement called it "a good light-hearted read". The Yorkshire Evening Post said: "Ten out of ten".
ISBN 1899807 26 8
Price £7.99
Format 129mm x 198mm
Paperback
Pagination 256

Test Cricket Grounds

John Woods

For dedicated cricket fans who plan to watch their country play overseas. Woods spent a year and a day visiting all 58 grounds that stage Test cricket. Wisden International Cricket magazine called it "a bible for the Barmy Army... perfect..."
ISBN 1899807 20 9

Price £12.99
Format 125mm x 217mm
Paperback
Pagination 480p all colour

Arthur Lydiard - Master Coach
Garth Gilmour
Arthur Lydiard was probably the most successful and influential running coach of the twentieth century. Garth Gilmour, Lydiard's close friend for more than 40 years, tells for the first time the full story of the coach's amazing career, often in Lydiard's own words.
Athletics Weekly said: "a perfect tribute to an immense genius".
ISBN 1899807 22 5
Price £17.99
Format 234mm x 153mm
Hardback
Pagination 256

International Rugby Who's Who
Andy Smith
This book provides all the fan needs to know about those who play the game and coach at the top level from the Zurich Premiership and Heineken Cup to the Super 12.
"An essential handbook... well produced," said the BBC.
ISBN 1899807 23 3
Price £17.95
Format 148mm x 210mm
Paperback
Pagination 428 all colour

Raich Carter – the biography

Frank Garrick

Raich Carter is the only man to win FA Cup winners' medals before and after the Second World War. Published to commemorate the 10th anniversary of his death. The Times said: "leaves the reader in no doubt about the nature of Carter's genius".
ISBN 1899807 18 7
Price £16.99
Format 155mm x 235mm
Hardback
Pagination 232

Phil Tufnell's AtoZ of Cricket

Phil Tufnell with Adam Hathaway

Phil Tufnell, one of cricket's most irreverent and well loved characters, now retired and a TV celebrity. The Cricket Magazine said: "a laugh on every page".
ISBN 1899807 17 9
Price £8.99
Format 130mm x 198mm
Paperback
Pagination 224